SAFETY, RISK AND ADVENTURE IN OUTDOOR ACTIVITIES

SAFETY, RISK AND ADVENTURE IN OUTDOOR ACTIVITIES

Bob Barton

Los Angeles | London | New Delhi
Singapore | Washington DC

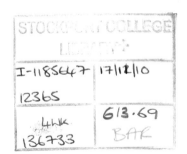
© Bob Barton 2007

First published 2007

Reprinted 2010

SAGE Publications Ltd
1 Oliver's Yard
55 City Road
London EC1Y 1SP

SAGE Publications Inc.
2455 Teller Road
Thousand Oaks, California 91320

SAGE Publications India Pvt Ltd
B 1/I 1 Mohan Cooperative Industrial Area
Mathura Road, New Delhi 110 044
India

SAGE Publications Asia-Pacific Pte Ltd
33 Pekin Street #02-01
Far East Square
Singapore 048763

Library of Congress Control Number: 2006928079

A catalogue record for this book is available from the British Library

ISBN 13 978-1-4129-2077-3
ISBN 13 978-1-4129-2078-0 (pbk)

All photographs by Bob Barton
Typeset by Pantek Arts Ltd, Maidstone, Kent
Printed in Great Britain by Ashford Colour Press Ltd, Gosport, Hampshire.

Contents

Acknowledgments

I have learned a great deal from those with whom I have climbed, walked, skied, sailed and, occasionally, paddled. I am grateful to them all for their impressive enthusiasm. Particularly memorable adventures were in the company of Allen Fyffe, Sam Crymble, Keith Geddes, Dave Morris, Jon Prosser, Mark Diggins, Steve Jones, Iain Peter, Mark Seaton, Brian Griffiths, John Cardy, Harold Gillespie, the late Peter Boardman and the late John Furness.

My career with the Outward Bound Trust has evolved into one where risk management is its prominent part. I admire Outward Bound's policy of openness on safety issues and acknowledge my debt of gratitude to that organisation and its superb staff. Previously, my colleagues, both at Glenmore Lodge and Brathay, gave a developing instructor much to aspire to, and my fellow mountain guides are continuing exemplars of effective risk management in action.

My thanks are due to Sir Michael Hobbs for his encouragement in the early stages of this book; to Sir Chris Bonington for unquenchable enthusiasm and wise counsel; to the late Fred Harper who showed how adventure and professionalism can be combined; and to Barbara Roscoe who opened my eyes to outdoor education.

Doug Jones, Rachel Carroll and Anne Salisbury kindly commented on an early draft and Johan Hovelynk, Jim Rowe, Jarkko Riikonen, Jorge Lantero, Mark Squires, Darren Black and Admiral Thiruchandran all gave insights into adventure education in other countries.

Thanks are due to the following individuals and organisations for permission to reproduce copyright material:

- ▶ Professor James Reason
- ▶ Simon Knight and Dave Anderson
- ▶ The Adventure Activities Licensing Authority
- ▶ East Barnby Outdoor Education Centre
- ▶ Canadian Mountain Holidays
- ▶ The Outward Bound Trust.

Other sources and influences are acknowledged in the text. I have benefited from the views and ideas of many people but any errors in what follows are mine alone.

Without the enduring support of Anna, Alex, Eliane and Flora the book would never have been written – thank you!

Foreword

SIR CHRIS BONINGTON

My life was changed completely when I discovered rock climbing at the age of sixteen. It gave me so much – the athletic joy of controlling muscle and mind to climb a stretch of rock, the stimulus of calculating risk, the sense of exploration, the wonder at the beauty of the natural environment and the friendships built from shared commitment and experience. Those feelings are as strong now as they were fifty-five years ago.

I also saw how much this exposure to adventure could do for other young people when I spent two years as an instructor at the Army Outward Bound School. I learnt the extent of the responsibility that I had as an instructor and the challenge of offering an enriching adventurous experience while at the same time ensuring that the risk to the student was kept to acceptable levels. This balance is not an easy one to achieve.

Bob Barton is particularly well qualified to help us to ensure that balance between the thrill of adventure and the need for a safe outcome. He is an outstanding mountaineer with a series of challenging first ascents in the Himalayas, an experienced mountain guide, a former instructor at Glenmore Lodge and Principal at Outward Bound Eskdale. I chair Outward Bound's Risk Management Committee, of which Bob is secretary. We have had many great days together on the hills and have discussed at length many of the topics covered in this book.

Adventure in the outdoors has so much to offer and this book will help you to enjoy it yourself and introduce it to others in the best possible way.

Chapter 1

Introduction

The case for outdoor adventure and the need for risk management

Generation upon generation of our ancestors lived freely upon the earth in forest and desert, tundra and savannah, the survival of the species, of their small bands, utterly dependent on the skill and enterprise of individuals and small groups. Life revolved and evolved around seeking shelter, finding food plants, hunting, fishing. Imagine the hunter poised, spear in hand, at one with the forest, a prey animal in view; the hunter completely engaged with his own destiny, a free agent aware of every sense and every muscle, totally absorbed in the moment when the spear is released.

Life has become constrained, controlled and commoditised to a point where many have forgotten what it is like to have this intensity of experience with nature, with oneself. Such moments are often called peak experiences and it is no coincidence that the metaphor draws on the ancient and powerful symbol of the mountain, the epitome of wilderness, of challenging, elusive but desirable goals.

The symbol of mountains: the summit of Castor, Zermatt.

As an adolescent, my own life was so transformed by an encounter with crags and mountains that, it seems to me now, most of the truly valuable lessons that I learnt came, not from a good education and a good family, but from this exciting hands-on school of climbing. Any sense of aesthetics that I possess has grown from travel in dramatic landscapes, an instinctive sense of ecology from upland habitats and an affinity for the literature of challenge from the urge to make sense of the intensity of my own experience. But these are merely valuable by-products beside the glowing core of self-knowledge and self-reliance that grew from the adventure itself.

This first experience has completely shaped the rest of my life. I still have a passion for the mountains and am lucky enough to have been able to make my career in adventure, yet many people whose experience of rock climbing or kayaking or sailing has been limited to a few intense hours still look back on these as a touchstone of adventurous experience, of life as it might be lived.

Adventure education can change lives, can intensify experience and extend its ripples far into a life. But its purpose is not to make lifetime sailors or skiers, climbers or paddlers, any more than the purpose of an education in literature is primarily to produce novelists or that in music to produce composers. A knowledge of all of these opens the doors of perception; a life denied music, literature and adventure is a life sold short.

Journeying is a great experience for youngsters.

Education in music and in literature may each have its own difficulties, but there is little doubt that the future of adventure education is under threat from a misapprehension of risk, its importance and its management. This book aims to help adventurous opportunities, especially those for young people, to flourish despite frequent hostility in the prevailing climate of opinion.

Public expectations and risk aversion

We are exposed to risk from the moment of our conception to our death. Although, in the developed world, knowledge and technology enable us to control, or at least defend against, the external hazards of climate, disease and starvation more effectively than ever before, we are, paradoxically, becoming more and more risk averse. It is easy to swallow the worm of thinking that the elimination of gratuitous risk can only be for the good but there is a hidden hook.

At an individual level many of us remember as the intense high points of life the occasions when we have faced and overcome great difficulties. Few would doubt that many of our most valuable lessons have grown from uncertainty and anxiety. Where would we be, what flaccid personalities would we have become, if all that discomfort, ambiguity and uncertainty had been removed at source?

For society as a whole there will always be a need for adventurousness of thought, deed and outlook. If we bring up children to believe that physical, emotional or intellectual risks are to be avoided we can hardly be surprised if the future does not bring successors to Captain Cook, to Darwin and to Shakespeare.

Others have written more eloquently about the philosophical and societal pitfalls of the apparently desirable elimination of risk. This book concerns itself with the more prosaic matter of the provision of outdoor activities and experiences. To set the ascent of a few hills against the wider decline of adventurousness may seem faintly ridiculous, yet those who journey in wilderness, who climb or sail, are privileged to enjoy an unrivalled practical training in risk management. We become expert in the necessary balancing act between what is desirable and what is reasonably possible to an extent where the balancing itself becomes central.

All of life is uncertain, but the engine of public opinion is inconsistent in its judgement of risk. Risks which are at a very low level, such as that from Creuzfeld-Jacob Disease, can be fanned into major public concern while daily exposure to very much higher levels of real risk do not attract proportionally greater concern. One must be sympathetic to the genuinely unfortunate individuals who find themselves the victims of statistically unlikely risks, but such sympathy does not necessarily lead to sound public policy.

We all deplore serious accidents in adventure activities or in any out of school learning. Such events, mercifully rare, justifiably raise great public concern and highlight the need for teachers, instructors and providers continually to aspire to the highest standards of risk management, but a public obsession with safety and blame and an ever greater aversion to any kind of risk threatens the availability of adventure in any meaningful form. The waste of young lives through lack of purpose and lack of self-esteem barely registers on the scale of public concern, yet many see this as the direct corollary of a diminution in the availability of opportunities for self-discovery, self-expression and self-belief. I do not pretend that outdoor experiences are the only remedy here, simply that they are too valuable, of too great a proven effect, to be rejected or neglected.

Adventure activities are certainly not entirely risk free, nor should they be. Robin Hodgkin wrote:

> Columbus set out to discover a new route to China … but he discovered America. Adventure rarely reaches its pre-determined goal.

This serves as a reminder of the essential unpredictability of genuine adventure. People seem increasingly to expect an outdoor experience to be a risk-free, error-free and controlled commodity like a pack of computer disks. Without uncertainty of outcome, without risk, we may have a very fine recreational experience, but we no longer have adventure.

We may be in danger of risk being sidelined as an undesirable by-product of adventure activity, of it being treated as the carcinogen to be eliminated from an otherwise healthy diet, rather than being recognised as itself an essential nutrient.

The balancing of risk and benefit has always been at the core of the long tradition of outdoor learning, but in many cases this balance seems to be under threat of replacement by the virtual elimination of risk. Colin Mortlock described a continuum of outdoor activity:

- Recreation

- Adventure

- Misadventure

and argued persuasively that the maximum educational benefit was to be found in the central sector or, more exactly, at the point of transition between adventure and misadventure. We are in danger of polarising both the operation and the perception of outdoor activity into either Recreation or Misadventure and losing the essential, productive but difficult middle ground.

Recreation, as defined in this context and typified by a leisurely walk in a beautiful park, can give great pleasure but, in Mortlock's model, is not likely to bring the deep experiences, the revelations that are to be found in genuine adventure.

John Adams of University College London has, in his book *Risk*, thrown light on different attitudes to risk. He identifies a 'Formal' sector of risk management (government, commerce, industry, 'experts' in general) whose objective is to *reduce* risk and an 'Informal' sector (everybody else) who:

> … go about the business of life – eating, drinking, loving, hating, walking, driving, saving, investing, working, socialising – striving for health, wealth and happiness in a world they know to be uncertain. The objective of these risk managers is to balance risks and rewards.

Tolerable risk or zero risk?

I prefer the term 'risk management' to that of 'safety' to describe what outdoor leaders and their managers do, because the former term, to my mind, carries a suggestion of a process committed to this essential balancing of risk and reward, of safety and adventure. In contrast, 'safety' seems to define the task too simply as the elimination of accident, with no consideration of benefit or balance. However, whatever term we use, it is imperative on us to avoid gratuitous risk when responsible for other people, and most especially when responsible for other people's children. Alongside this we must be honest that we are often dealing with actual risk, albeit risk limited to a tolerable level, but emphatically not a position of zero risk, or of risk that is entirely 'perceived'. It helps nobody to claim inaccurately that 'our activities are completely safe'.

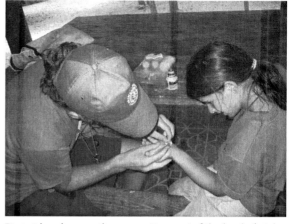

First aid and sympathy – a routine part of the leader's job.

Adult practitioners of adventure sports can and should make their own decisions concerning the level of risk with which they are willing to engage and which they regard as tolerable for their own activities, but the margin of safety must be higher when, for instance, we are acting *in loco parentis*. This is discussed more fully in Chapter 14 but, for now, it will suffice to emphasise that risk management is our most effective lever of control over this margin and on the underlying balance between risk and security.

To win the trust of parents and their children, outdoor providers must demonstrate that they have expertise in the balancing act of risk and reward to such an extent that they can provide intense developmental experiences at a level of actual risk that is generally regarded as tolerable. This is why we need to be very good at managing risks – not only to reduce the risk of accidents but also to avoid killing the adventure. If providers are pushed into a corner where every sprained ankle results in an inquiry and a legal claim, it may become impossible to retain the illuminating spark of adventure.

It is now widely recognised that the provision of adventurous activities can be harnessed as a highly effective vehicle for learning about teamwork, about leadership, about personal interaction. It is also an unrivalled vehicle for learning the key life skill of balancing risk against opportunity.

By putting active risk management at the heart of adventure we can give young people a superb arena in which to develop their skills in managing the uncertainties of life, but only if we leave enough uncertainty of outcome in the process for their risk management to be real. We should aim to provide:

- better education in life skills;

- an improved ability of participants to manage risks in their own lives;

- real adventure.

All over the country, just as generations of developing adults did before them, there are groups of young people desperately trying to have an adventure that speaks to them. Too often their efforts are frustrated by regulation, inappropriate intervention and lack of imagination from those who see themselves as responsible for the control of such creative expression. Those in charge have become so transfixed by the possibility of risk that they are in danger of throwing out the educational baby with the bathwater of risk avoidance. Not long ago I heard of a typical example where a group of seventeen year olds undertaking a four-day exploration journey were so constrained by the rigid timetable and regime of reporting applied 'in the interests of safety' that their opportunities for discovery and adventure were subsumed into a sterile exercise of box ticking. Nobody was hurt, but what exactly is the point of such an experience?

Real adventure

Adventure is powerful stuff. 'Challenge', 'achievement', 'conquest' and 'drama' are some of the more grandiose elements of its language and perhaps the ones most likely to capture our imagination. But we must not forget the darker side where uncertainty, discomfort and danger can threaten. Challenge can be sterile without uncertainty of outcome and many feel that the darker side cannot be evaded without corrupting the ideal and purpose of adventuring. In a holistic view of adventure the attractive and threatening elements are in balance and harmony as yin is to yang.

Adventure – the word outcrops everywhere in the landscape of outdoor education. My thesaurus tells me that it is synonymous with:

- escapade
- exploit
- quest
- venture
- exciting activity
- exploration
- voyage.

The senses of 'exploration' and 'voyage' will resonate with outdoor educationalists but most would add a need for uncertainty of outcome. A routine voyage on a commercial ferry would rarely qualify as adventure yet the same journey by different means, in a small dinghy for instance, certainly would.

In politics and business, an 'adventure' is something to be avoided; the term is a pejorative one. In the narrower field of outdoor education, adventure is usually regarded as a core asset, something to be applauded and promoted yet, in modern life, the same term seems to be applicable to playing a computer game or tasting a new flavour of yoghurt.

Real adventure – imaginative instruction gives a great session on a very wet day.

One of the most important ingredients of a memorable adventure is the combination of some uncertainty of outcome and the possibility of significantly adverse consequences in the event of an unfavourable result. Many computer games can grip the player but failure carries few consequences – and one can always switch off the machine. The need for commitment, a degree of inescapability, is another desirable ingredient.

Adventure education and outdoor education are often used synonymously alongside other terms such as outdoor learning and the recent introduction of 'out of classroom learning'. Drawing boundary lines is not necessarily productive but some of these umbrella terms cover a very broad range of worthwhile undertakings from a visit to the botanical gardens through to a three-week kayak expedition along the coast of Greenland. It is a topic of debate whether all such activities are equally worthwhile or whether the component of adventure is one to be valued above others.

Using broad classifications may give a misleading impression of the degree to which children are given the opportunity to engage with 'real' adventure. If a walk in the park is officially regarded as offering many of the same benefits as a more laborious adventure, such as canoeing the River Spey from source to mouth, then it becomes increasingly difficult to justify the effort, the expense and the intrinsically greater risks of the more challenging option. Why not save on the travel and staffing costs and do the whole thing in the classroom via virtual reality?

Simon Knight and Dave Anderson comment:

> With self-esteem as the goal, Government-sponsored Outdoor Adventure has a much narrowed focus and in fact loses its adventure agenda altogether. The necessity for esteem-generating guaranteed success results in the abolition of potential failure. What's left is outdoor banality, boredom within the 'comfort zone'. In circumstances of constant success, young people also derive an unrealistic opinion of their abilities. Failure is an important rendezvous with reality and acts as a spur to improve oneself next time.

My own working definition of real adventure includes the following key features:

- some uncertainty of outcome and content – we do not know quite where it will lead;
- wild, dramatic or unusual settings that are part of nature;
- an active rather than a passive engagement with the activity;
- an intrinsic level of challenge. Problems to be solved in order to reach the desired outcome and the undertaking feels 'difficult' but not 'impossible';
- direct and immediate consequences attach to completion or non-completion – we might get cold or wet, tired or hungry if we do not succeed;
- participants have personal responsibility for the outcome – 'we did it ourselves';
- speaks to the soul – how can anything so life enhancing do otherwise?

Although solo adventures are an impressive part of the canon, most adventure education takes place through small groups – big enough to give interaction but small enough to give everyone a chance to contribute to the outcome. This gives an added dimension of group working, which many would add to the list above.

Exceptions to the list can certainly be identified. I was once taken on a journey crawling through the flues and chambers of a huge (and fortunately disused) iron smelter that seemed highly adventurous, a kind of urban caving that was emphatically not part of nature. However, my enthusiasm for adventure would be tempered if it became a predominantly industrial activity without the magic of sunrise, stars and the sweep of wild country.

If we revisit the spectrum ranging from the kayak expedition to the botanical gardens we might regard the range as representing, at one end, in the kayaks, the characteristics of adventure listed above. At the other, we see an approach that is more specific, and more recognisable as having affinities to classroom learning, so that we might regard it as an outdoor classroom with for instance an intention to teach about conifers or Linnaean classification. A comparison of key features might be as listed in Table 1.1.

Table 1.1 Comparison of key features

Outdoor classroom	Adventure education
Defined content and outcome	Some, possibly large, uncertainty of outcome and content
Settings that are part of nature	Wild, dramatic or unusual settings that are part of nature
Engagement with the activity may be passive	An active rather than a passive engagement with the activity
Problem-solving may be needed in order to reach the desired outcome	An intrinsic level of challenge, presenting problems to be solved in order to reach the desired outcome
Consequences are likely to be experienced at a later time	Direct and immediate consequences attach to completion or non-completion
Participants have personal responsibility for their own learning	Participants have personal responsibility for the outcome
Speaks to the intellect	Speaks to the soul

It is useful to decide where a particular activity lies on the spectrum between the two limits depicted in the table. I of course recognise that inspired teachers may make involvement in the outdoor classroom both active and inspiring!

Outdoor education is usually strongly aligned to experiential learning and we often see two different approaches to 'processing' the outdoor experience. One camp asserts that 'the mountains should be allowed to speak for themselves', that if an adventure experience is sufficiently real and intense, those taking part will inevitably take on the most relevant lessons. In this approach, the leader is primarily a guide and technical resource.

In contrast, the other school of thought advocates much more intervention in the learning process, with leaders facilitating the identification and transfer of learning from the outdoor experience. This is done by means of reflection, review, and reapplication, in line with the learning cycle described by Kolb and others. This is usually done by rolling through an iterative loop of Experiencing – Reviewing – Concluding – Planning, or in its simplest form:

Most outdoor education includes a significant component of facilitation, but many practitioners feel it to be important that facilitation does not eclipse the opportunity for real adventure. A balance must again be drawn.

Comparison with other fields

The perception of risk in adventure activities does not always tally with the reality, even for those who take part. Knight and Anderson further describe a phenomenon that will be recognised by every outdoor leader who has worked with kids:

> Parents are understandably concerned about their child's safety – but perceptions and reality often diverge. Listening to children's stories develop on the minibus going home, you would think that death had been but a whisker away – parents' jaws must drop when they hear the child's version of events. But here's the secret: outdoor adventure has the potential to be dangerous but is in fact very safe. Because of the potential for accidents workers have always assessed risk with a view to being safe.

There are enough uncertain variables to make it very difficult to compare overall safety in outdoor education with that in everyday life. Official accident statistics are often based on figures relating to death, because a fatality is a definite statistical event that must be reported under law. This means that national statistical records tend to be much more reliable for deaths than for, say, serious injury. Prepare for a gloomy interlude.

Every year in Great Britain about 13,000 people are killed in accidents of all kinds. More than 3,500 of the total are as a result of road traffic accidents, which are the most important cause of accidental death for those under 45 years of age, and more than 4,000 occur in the home or in the garden. Of the total number of accidental deaths about 1,000 are children.

By making a number of assumptions, it is possible to make an analysis which indicates that the average risk of death for young people during a day of adventure activities is roughly the same as that for an average day in the rest of their lives, in and out of school. The risk of death, by any cause, for a particular child on any given day is about 1 in 5 million.

Stepping back to a wider view, the annual rate of accidental death during planned out-of-school activities is about three or four per annum from a population of 10 million British children. It should be remembered that the underlying risks of say, illness or road traffic accident still apply during these out-of-school activities and the fatalities that do occur during outdoor sessions may be unconnected with the activity itself.

These figures give no support to a view that outdoor education is an unreasonably dangerous activity. Serious accidents may happen, but in the broad picture, the level of risk is very similar to that in everyday life. Practitioners would argue that the benefits are inestimably greater.

The Department for Education and Skills in a recent memorandum to a House of Lords' Inquiry into the Government's Policy on Risk Management commented:

> Educational visits of a less naturally hazardous nature – the huge majority – are also thriving. These are mainly cultural and sporting activities. They carry their own risks, of course, and these are safely managed by thousands of teachers and other school staff for curricular purposes. While millions of pupils take part in such activities every year, the chances of a serious incident are very low indeed – about 0.5 in a million. We know of only 26 accidental deaths of pupils from schools in England since 1997. (All but one of them occurred on out-of-classroom activities, only one of those – the recent tragic death of a 14 year old pupil whilst caving with his school in North Yorkshire – on a higher-hazard activity.)

Tom Price was one of my predecessors at Outward Bound® Eskdale, and is a man with a unique ability to get to the essence of a thing. Two of his statements seem particularly apposite:

> Anyone can make adventure training safe by taking all the adventure out of it.

> The best safety lies not so much in the avoidance of danger, but in learning how to deal with it.

My opinion is that the combination of these two ideas is strong persuasion for the need to have risk, or, more exactly, the active management and balancing of risk and opportunity by participants, at the centre of outdoor education.

Perhaps we need to see the right to adventure as a fundamental human right. The safety argument, at times, seems all pervasive and it is not impossible to imagine a future time when anybody engaging with anything other than a trivial level of risk will be seen as betraying the norms, or even the laws, of society. Do we really want a society which outlaws adventure?

Chapter summary

- Adventure is life enhancing.

- Rampant risk aversion threatens its continued availability.

- There is a spectrum – Recreation : Adventure : Misadventure.

- Outdoor activities teach the key skill of risk management.

- Leaders must be skilful at balancing risk and benefit.

- Outdoor learning includes a wide range of approaches.

- Uncertainty of outcome and dramatic environments are two central features of adventure education.

- Out-of-school outdoor activities for children are, on average, no more dangerous than everyday life.

Chapter 2

Principles of outdoor risk management

There are a number of terms, concepts and principles that apply to the management of risk in adventure activities. Some of these apply equally to risk management in other fields and are drawn from the body of knowledge concerning safety management in industry and elsewhere.

Hazard and risk

In everyday life these terms are used loosely, with overlapping, almost synonymous meanings. Professionals concerned with risk management use them in a much more specific way and it is useful to understand the distinctions usually drawn.

A *hazard* is anything with the potential to cause harm (loss or injury). Examples of hazards in adventure activities include falls from height, drowning, falling objects, lightning strikes, equipment failure, assault, cold injury and many more. It is an unfortunate party that meets all of these on a single day.

Note that identifying the hazard alone does not directly tell us anything about the likelihood of occurrence of the possible harm, nor its possible severity, although in practice these may be quite apparent. All we know is that a hazard exists. The crater on Mount Etna during a period of volcanic activity undoubtedly contains many hazards which could injure or kill someone who goes there to explore. If I choose, instead, to stay away from the crater, then the risk to me of, say, falling into one of its hot shafts is effectively zero – but the hazard remains attached to Etna itself.

The severity of harm that may ensue when a certain hazard comes to bear gives us an important indication of how seriously we should take that hazard. To describe a hazard in this way, we may employ adjectives such as 'slight', 'moderate' or 'catastrophic'. So we may talk of a slight chance of moderate injury or a high danger of critical injury. We might describe falling into a red hot volcanic shaft as a catastrophic hazard, but would probably describe the rough, ankle-twisting ground on the ascent to the crater as a moderate hazard. In neither case does identification of the hazard tell us how likely we are to be injured – to do this we must consider risk itself.

Risk is a measure of the likelihood that a particular hazard will cause harm. It is affected by both the frequency of exposure to a hazard and the severity of the hazard itself. We really are asking:

- How often might we meet the hazard?
- How bad is it if we do?

Risk can be described qualitatively or quantitatively.

Qualitative descriptions of risk

These usually describe the level of risk by also drawing on an escalating string of adjectives such as insignificant, 'slight', 'moderate', 'significant' or 'high risk' and so on.

With all the available adjectives relating to hazards and risks, we should avoid becoming slaves to semantics but recognise instead that we are engaging our best efforts in trying to address the balance between opportunity and possible loss. Identifying and classifying risk is a worthwhile process, but the end result is only as useful as the effect it can have on our practical management of risks. How the risk was described and identified makes little immediate difference to the victim of a serious accident, though it may be highly significant at a later stage, such as during possible litigation.

It is clear to most people that a combination of frequent occurrence and severe consequence should ring very loud alarm bells. A teacher who allows a class of ten year olds to play, dodging large waves crashing regularly on to an undercut rock ledge would have allowed both frequency and severity to apply – and would be justifiably criticised in the event of a child being swept away.

An even more extreme example would be if an instructor chose to operate a beginners' rock climbing session on a steep ten-metre cliff without using ropes. The fact that slips by beginners are not at all uncommon, and that the consequence of such a slip from five metres or more would be severe, explains why no reputable provider adopts such an uncontrollable (and unjustifiable) approach.

Frequent incidences with slight consequences can, in most situations, be considered an entirely tolerable risk, we might even say a trivial risk. The risk of a broken fingernail while operating a sailing dinghy is unlikely to be seen as a reason for a provider to remove sailing from the activity menu or for an individual to avoid taking part.

Of course each individual has different priorities and, occasionally, some circumstance will render an activity unsuitable. A model for hand cosmetics or a professional violinist may both find a broken nail a very strong deterrent to taking part in the sailing session, though, of course, neither would be likely to consider that their lives were being put at risk. I would not expect a provider to warn me that I might break my fingernail – we must surely see this as part of the general wear and tear of bumps and scrapes that physical activity inevitably entails.

Infrequent occurrences with slight consequences are by definition trivial. No reasonable person could expect a school to have a policy to deal with such things.

Decision-making when risks are judged as very high or very low is relatively simple (simple but not easy) – it is usually clear to any competent person that things are either unacceptably dangerous or that risk is at a trivial level. The greatest difficulty for providers of adventure activities who are dealing with a wide spectrum of possible risk is in the area where actual harm could result and where risks might be judged as 'moderate'. There is no quick solution, so careful consideration must be give to the factors outlined in the section below on how safe should safe be.

The risk spectrum

Figure 2.1 gives a sense of the spectrum of risk. It is included mainly to stimulate critical thinking about how you should regard the risks which you have to manage. It is obvious that everything depends on what meaning is given to individual terms such as 'moderate' or 'high'.

		Severity of harm			
		Catastrophic	*Critical*	*Moderate*	*Slight*
	Frequent	**HIGH RISK**	**HIGH RISK**	**SERIOUS RISK**	**Moderate risk**
Frequency of occurrence	*Likely*	**HIGH RISK**	**HIGH RISK**	**SERIOUS RISK**	**Moderate risk**
	Occasional	**HIGH RISK**	**SERIOUS RISK**	**Moderate risk**	**Low risk**
	Unlikely	**SERIOUS RISK**	**Moderate risk**	**Moderate risk**	**Low risk**
	Remote	**Moderate or low risk**	**Moderate or low risk**	**Low risk**	**Low risk**

Figure 2.1 The risk spectrum

As a broad generalisation, situations of high and serious risk are not acceptable in the provision of outdoor activities and programmes, except in very specialised circumstances, such as in the case of informed and experienced adults who have willingly entered into a risky undertaking – for example an ascent of a Himalayan peak. This takes us into the territory of risk contracts and the acknowledgement of risk – further discussed in Chapter 14. These comments are confined to *provided* programmes –

Coastal traversing – great fun until the big wave arrives
… so where are we on the risk spectrum?

individuals operating independently and not offering services to others are usually free to make their own decisions, though would be wise to consider exactly what they are taking on.

Correspondingly, activities accurately assessed as low risk would be considered to be acceptable in almost all cases and should probably describe the great majority of activities undertaken by a particular organisation or leader.

As implied above, almost all of the difficulty of management, and a deal of professional interest, lies in the zone of moderate risk. If anything is assessed as other than low risk then careful case by case analysis is needed. We should not simply blunder into a situation of higher risk without heeding the possible consequences.

So how safe should safe be?

There is no absolute standard of safety and one person's misadventure is another's gentle recreation. To simply ask this question is an excellent starting point for making good choices about a particular individual or group. The answer can only come from a process which:

- Assesses the client group:
  - adult or minor
  - level of experience of the activity
  - physical ability
  - attitude to risk
  - resilience
  - expectations.

- Assesses the activity:
  - level of risk
  - level of difficulty and challenge
  - protection arrangements
  - match to the client's capabilities and expectations
  - expertise and experience of leader in that activity.

- Assesses the location:
  - remoteness and access to help
  - expected conditions and weather
  - match to the client's capabilities and expectations
  - previously used by leader?

- Assesses the degree of supervision:
  - proximity of instructor
  - supervisor/participant ratio
  - experience of staff
  - availability of competent assistance
  - expertise and experience of leader.

During an activity session it can be illuminating to imagine ourselves on a line which at one end has a virtually guaranteed level of safety and at the other a high level of risk. It is obvious that the limits at either end of this line vary from activity to activity, but in all cases it is worthwhile for instructors to have an awareness of where on the line they and their charges are at a particular moment. A common situation leading to loss is an unnoticed escalation of the level of risk with which the party is engaging.

Getting the balance right

It is clear that clients will have varying expectations of what is tolerable risk. A group of young mountain bikers who are taking up snow boarding are likely to be fit, 'up for it' and willing to take some real risks in the new sport; a middle-aged person recovering from illness and using hill walking as a way back to fitness is unlikely to welcome an aggressive pace or an apparently careless approach to risk.

When I was a young activity instructor an old hand said to me 'When you are working with clients and you have two alternatives, always choose the safer one.' I have come to learn that, unfortunately, things are not always quite so clear cut. The advice is, on the face of it, perfectly sound and widely applicable, but if we always choose the 'safer' option we are in danger of losing the spark of adventure. Travelling by car may be a safer choice (though that is arguable!) for the journey than walking the Coast to Coast Walk, but who could claim that it is more rewarding?

A skilled instructor has the judgement to make this balancing act work but newer leaders can get into difficulties if they choose an exciting and challenging option without having considered the possible consequences. We have to take particular care to be sure of our justification when we are taking what might be considered by some to be a more risky option. I suggest that the advice to would be leaders might be given a more relevant slant if we were to say:

> When you are working with clients and have not chosen the safer alternative, think of how, in the worst case, you would justify your choice to the Coroner's Court.

Worst case analysis is a useful tool for any decision-maker. It does not mean that we think there is any real chance of a fatality, but does help us to focus critical analysis on the important decisions.

Quantitative descriptions of risk

Quantitative or numerical measures give an impression of great precision but this can disguise what is often a lack of useful content.

For example, a statement such as 'Men aged 35–44 have an annual risk of death from all causes of 1 in 590' takes an overview of an entire population and gives a numerical indication of risk. While of great interest, particularly to men in that age range, this tells us little about the risks faced by a particular individual, who may be a couch potato, a trained athlete or an individual with a penchant for a particularly hazardous activity such as cave diving. What the bald statement means is that, on average, if we find 590 men in the stated age range, after one year, one of them will have died. A gambler might say that the odds of death during a single year are 590 to 1 for a man in this age range.

It is unusual for adventure activity providers to have access to useful public information concerning numerical risks for outdoor activities and, as mentioned previously, such information is often confined to statistics about death. We should recognise that fatality rates do not generally give useful guidance to those managing the risks of outdoor activities because they describe very infrequent and often atypical events.

Larger-scale providers can generate a database containing a wider range of incidents and this can start to give valuable information about rates and patterns of occurrence and how best to manage specific situations in future. This topic is explored further in Chapter 13, but it is worth mentioning here that some of the most useful indicators are those of the trend and ranking of reports. For instance, if we detect a large increase in the rate of occurrence of scalding during camp cooking we need to focus attention on how to reduce its occurrence. Similarly, finding that the most likely cause of serious incidents is common assault tells us that we need to address the problem of conflict and aggressive behaviour as a matter of priority.

Uncontrollable hazards

The Office of National Statistics gives the annual risk of death from lightning in England and Wales as 1 in 15 million. This is a low level of occurrence of what is literally a 'bolt from the blue' and few would dispute that lightning is a good example of an uncontrollable hazard.

However, three groups appear to feature prominently in the statistics for lightning strikes – anglers and golfers (who each wave metal or carbon conducting rods in the air) and hill walkers, whose frequent aim is to be above all surrounding land.

So it is clear that, although we may not be able to prevent a lightning strike, we can certainly influence our exposure to it, and that is the key to managing uncontrollable hazards. Mountaineers cannot prevent ice falling from seracs but they can avoid the areas raked by ice debris, or, if this is impossible, at least travel at maximum speed to reduce exposure. Sailors may not be able to weather a hurricane, but they can avoid known storm tracks and periods of frequent or forecast occurrence and so on.

Actual and perceived risk

Within adventure activities a distinction is often drawn between 'actual' or real risk and 'perceived' or apparent risk. This distinction does not really stand up to detailed examination because in any activity, even the most innocuous, there is likely to be a small residual level of risk that could result in loss or injury. However, it does usefully separate activities such as ocean sailing or alpine mountaineering, where there is an inevitable level of actual risk, no matter how competent and well equipped are the party, and activities such as a high ropes course, which, if competently designed, built and operated, carries only a very small level of residual risk but a very high component of thrill and challenge – which we call perceived risk.

The crucial difference is that an error by the participant on the high ropes (a situation of perceived risk) will be much less likely to have serious consequences than one made on the deck of a sailing boat in mid Atlantic – where the risks are real.

In general terms, large-scale, far-ranging activities:

- are more complex, with more to go wrong;
- tend to put those taking part more at the mercy of nature and further from assistance;
- often have a significant exposure to uncontrollable hazards;
- are more likely to entail actual risk.

Examples of these activities would include:

- sea kayak journeys;
- coastal and offshore sailing;
- winter mountaineering;
- ski mountaineering.

Experience is at a huge premium for leaders in activities of this kind, because the proven way to deal successfully with highly complex and variable situations is to have already developed appropriate generic skills in countless other comparable situations.

In contrast, the more confined activities are generally easier to control because they:

Ski mountaineering – a magnificent but committing activity. The evidence of previous avalanches indicates that we are probably dealing with a situation of actual risk.

- are less complex and so may be less uncertain and more controllable;
- are close to assistance and external supervision;
- have little exposure to uncontrollable hazards;
- may have few actual risks (though the opposite may be true).

Examples of these might include:

- lawn games;
- running a zip wire;
- climbing on a climbing wall;
- raft building on a confined body of water.

At their simplest, the more confined activities can be adequately operated with a narrow set of skills and limited previous experience, so reasonably able and sensible instructors can be specifically trained and authorised to lead the activity in a relatively short time. To be successful we would normally expect the

Spider's web: a fun activity that needs teamwork and planning. Although a controllable situation of relatively low risk, there is residual actual risk, such as if the person being supported is dropped to the ground.

training to be set up and delivered by a person of wider experience and greater expertise who would be able to recognise and communicate any pitfalls.

When we apply the general principles of risk to real, practical situations we are engaging in a process of risk assessment. This is covered in Chapter 6.

Where to focus our attention?

One would expect that those who are responsible for others in adventurous environments, who regularly balance their duties of care against a passionate desire to pass on the sacred flame of adventure, to be unchallenged experts in the difficult balance of risk and security. Perhaps we are, but it seems possible that we have allowed the combined effects of an exaggerated fear of litigation and the influence of a systems-focused approach to regulation to deflect us from what we are good at and to persuade us to chase the wrong hare.

Stated simply, the danger is that increasingly we build systems and controls that shift attention away from the critical importance of human error and human fallibility. Let me give an example. Ropes courses have been a popular component of adventure programmes for more than fifty years. Participants follow a high-level constructed path, with some protection against the possibility of falling. This is often achieved by the use of 'cows' tails' – rope links with one end attached to the person, the other clipped to a protection cable. Until a few years ago, such courses had an improvised, sylvan appearance that many enjoyed, but this has been overtaken by a much more high-tech approach. Where once were only lash-

ings and spars are now to be seen pylons, stainless steel cables and shear reduction blocks. There are important side issues such as the avoidance of damage to trees and the reassuring appearance of such facilities to anxious clients, but I understand that the main thrust behind these expensive changes has been an admirable commitment to improve the safety of the activity.

It is certainly unclear whether the hundreds of thousands of pounds invested in such a way has had any proportional positive effect on the safety of those taking part. By far the most important threat to the safety of participants on

At the heart of the forest on this improvised ropes course – protection is by 'cows' tails'.

the usual form of ropes course is their own error in the clipping and unclipping of safety links or that of the instructor in setting up and supervising the activity. In most cases, the risk of the entire structure failing seems a less immediate threat.

Unfortunately, taking defensive action against human error is a more complex and difficult process than, for instance, strengthening a support cable, and may force us into the uncertain world of behavioural science rather than the concrete realities of engineering. We might estimate that errors in clipping are many times more likely to cause serious injury than structural failure and yet deploy our resources in the reverse of this proportion, largely because changing the behaviour of people is difficult. (I should point out that, for the example chosen, clipping errors can be effectively addressed by engineering solutions, albeit rather expensive ones. However, these 'continuous rail' systems are not in widespread use. The general point still applies.)

Inspection

Heisenberg's Principle indicated that for sub-atomic particles, just by being there, an observer distorts the system and makes things behave differently. Inspectors tend to inspect what can be readily inspected and this can, in turn, distort the way providers operate. I have now seen a number of Adventure Activities Licensing Authority (AALA) inspections and nearly every one has included a request to see the logging and recording system for climbing ropes. Nobody pretends that such a system is likely materially to improve the safety of participants, since, for all practical purposes, climbing ropes simply do not break, especially during the kind of use that most outdoor centres make of them. So why is it done? AALA inspectors do a very competent job within the limited time available to them for an inspection, but if they are frequently focusing attention on inessentials there is a danger that outdoor providers start to behave as though those inessentials are the core of effective risk management. I believe that outdoor providers need forcibly to reject a mechanistic view of risk management and re-establish what our cumulative experience tells us – that it is addressing the possibility, indeed the inevitability, of human fallibility, variability and error that must be the cornerstone of our risk management.

The other growing influence (and this one seems largely malign), is the fear of litigation. I recently heard providers discussing whether they should keep participant disclaimers for five years or ten. It is hard to avoid the impression that outdoor operators are amassing filing cabinets full of this and similar stuff, which may have an importance in any subsequent litigation but which add precisely nothing to the safety of the clients in the field.

The precautionary principle

This principle is one that has recently gained great currency and which is often invoked in relation to the introduction of new technology, as in the case of genetically modified foods or health scares such as the outbreak of bovine spongiform encephalitis (BSE) in cattle.

At its simplest, the precautionary principle states that it is better to be safe than sorry. It places the burden of proof of the safety of anything new on to the innovator or developer. This is instead of there being a presumption that the innovation should proceed unless the public, or a special interest group, are able to demonstrate that it is unsafe or in some other way undesirable.

It seems hard to argue against the application of the precautionary principle, but there is a danger that, without appropriate rigour in the arguments and research, superficial objections or irrational fears can put near insuperable obstacles in the path of worthwhile technology. Some claim that the principle blocks action on the basis of what we do not know rather than what we do know.

The principle itself has little application to adventure activities but it does seem to contribute to a growing climate of risk aversion where safety is valued above all things. This climate is threatening to any form of education or experience where actual risk may be present. Proponents of adventure activities should be ready to show the other side of the coin, to communicate the tremendous benefits of adventure as a counter to the risks, which tend to have undue prominence in the public view.

Key features of outdoor risk management

When we look at what can affect the safety and success of an outdoor activity session we soon identify a great many diverse influences that might include:

- the quality and experience of the leader;
- the health and fitness of the participant;
- the quality of the equipment in use;
- the location used;
- the attitude to risk;
- the communication arrangements;
- the briefing of participants;
- the weather conditions;
- the availability of food and water;
- the identification and control of hazards.

The list can become almost endless. Fortunately, many of the necessary skills to manage these items have become second nature to experienced leaders. If we consider how we might monitor, control or utilise these influences to our benefit, we can broadly group them into:

- people
- culture
- systems.

We will examine each of these in turn in the following chapters.

Chapter summary

- A hazard is anything with the potential to cause harm.
- Risk is a measure of the likelihood that a particular hazard will cause harm.
- Risk can be described qualitatively or quantitatively.
- Providers should decide where they are, and where they should be, on the risk spectrum.
- The identification of *actual* or *perceived* risk is strongly influenced by the nature of the activity provided.
- Human error and human judgement are of central importance to effective risk management.

Chapter 3

People – the key influence

The two great variables in adventure activities are the uncertain environment in which we operate and the behaviour of people. Deeply inspiring or hugely frustrating, neither is ever entirely predictable.

Our capacity to influence the environment is limited and the ways in which we can react to its effect are discussed elsewhere. How the influence of staff and participants on safety is managed to best effect is one of the features that distinguishes top-quality providers from the rest.

Staff

Influence

Some years ago, I was involved in a pilot training event which aimed to help experienced instructors develop an even greater awareness of the processes governing judgement and decision-making in activities. We were seeking to put the group in unfamiliar situations close to the edge of their own 'comfort zones' in activities such as sea canoeing, and to then explore everyone's reactions.

On the day in question, the instructor in charge of the activity had to abandon our original plans for an open sea journey because of extremely high winds, forecast to reach a scary Force 10. I confess that I was, at first, unconvinced by his alternative proposal to go to the Menai Straits, a narrow channel between the mainland and the isle of Anglesey which is subject to powerful tidal streams reaching, at their peak, five knots or more.

It seemed to me that we were unlikely to get onto the water at all – a dull prospect but at least one that would allow us to consider the decision-making process and thus contribute something to the course aims.

In the event, the lead instructor took us to the launch point from where we could look out into the channel, an impressive place of cresting waves and wind driven spray. He presented a convincing case for launching and for making a journey that took into account the severe constraints of the weather and sea state, that was within the considerable capabilities of the group and that, most importantly, had a number of escape options.

Everyone agreed to this and we were off, hugging the shore. On a still day this journey, never more than ten metres from the shore, would have been trivial for a group of fairly strong paddlers like ours; in this gale of wind it was an exciting tightrope down a narrow band of shelter between the rocks of the shore and the raging waters of the main channel. Every few minutes an intense squall would bring us all together, clinging one to another in a supportive raft, until, once the squall passed, we could paddle again. All went smoothly and the trip was completed in great style, everyone euphoric at snatching an excellent adventure from a most unpromising situation – and with the bonus for our training of much material to discuss.

It was a great example of how a highly skilled and imaginative instructor can make the very best of a difficult situation and can establish exactly the right balance between adventure and security for that particular group on that particular day.

Staff are undoubtedly the greatest single influence on safety (and quality) in adventure activities. An instructor of the highest quality may still be able to run a successful and safe session even when

This instructor radiates experience of his working environment in the Northern forests.

constrained by poor equipment, adverse weather, inadequate documentation, unsuitable ratios and so on. This is, probably, not to be recommended, but any such success will always come from a recognition of the limitations to what can be reasonably attempted together with a proportionate scaling of one's plans.

Now consider the converse situation with a small group of well equipped participants enjoying, in perfect weather, a well known and well prepared activity supported by well documented risk assessments and procedures, but led by an inexperienced instructor unaware of his own limitations.

Which is the more worrying situation? Which is more likely to go badly wrong? When a head teacher, manager or youth worker is in the position of having responsibility for an activity session or a journey without immediate hands-on control, the most reassuring feature is always that of having a sound, sensible and experienced person in charge in the field. Preparation, planning, equipment, information flow are all extremely important but the experienced manager will always expect to be able to put his or her trust in the best leaders.

Since staff are the key influence, effective processes to select, train and authorise them should be at the heart of the management of adventure activities. This is a major, and by no means simple, responsibility for professional providers but is even more vital for voluntary or informal groups, who often have more limited access to some of the controls and processes available to their professional colleagues.

The leader's skills

It is important to remember that, to be successful, an outdoor leader needs to combine both technical skills and leadership skills, each at an appropriate level. Technical skills are those demanded by the complexities of the activity itself. For a skier they would include the ability to make a turn or to hold a ski edge on an icy traverse. For sailors, technical skills would include being able to rig the boat, to go about from one tack to the other, to retrieve a man overboard; for hill walkers, the ability to read a map and use a compass.

Some activities make considerable technical demands yet seem to involve relatively straightforward issues of leadership and control, others may not be unduly demanding of technical ability but may need inspired leadership. The most serious undertakings often combine both technical and leadership demands at high levels, but it must be recognised that, in any emergency situation, there will almost always be a need for leadership and for an ability to remain calm and objective in the face of the huge pressures and distractions that build with every passing second. Figure 3.1 shows some examples of activities which typically make differing technical and leadership demands.

HIGH TECHNICAL LOW LEADERSHIP	HIGH TECHNICAL HIGH LEADERSHIP
● Coaching adults in ski technique on a ski mat ● A climbing wall top rope session	● Offshore sailing ● An extended mountain bike journey
LOW TECHNICAL LOW LEADERSHIP	LOW TECHNICAL HIGH LEADERSHIP
● A picnic in the park ● Lawn games	● A cliff-top coastal walk ● Supervised games in a swimming pool for a group prone to challenging behaviour

Figure 3.1 Technical and leadership demands.

When an activity occupies the Low technical/Low leadership box we may now find ourselves in the recreational zone as described in Chapter 2.

These allocations are rather arbitrary and it can be argued that there is never an occasion when the leader cannot suddenly find that a change of circumstances has radically revised the priorities and the hazards to be managed and that high leadership skills are now needed.

Most teachers planning to lead a party of children on a simple countryside walk would be able to list, for example, appropriate actions in the event of an emergency, but when the actual crisis arrives, even the simplest of tasks like identifying a location or making a phone call can suddenly become desperately difficult. In such a situation it is the personal qualities that we usually associate with leadership that come to the fore.

In the lists above, 'man overboard' is mentioned as a technical skill that a competent sailor must have mastered. If during a dark, stormy night at sea the terrifying cry of 'man overboard' is heard, then the person in charge (who, of course, may not be the skipper if the skipper is overboard) undoubtedly needs to have boat handling skills, an understanding of the need for careful pinpointing of anyone in the water and how to retrieve a helpless person from the sea, but those skills are likely to have little value, or to be incorrectly applied, without an overarching ability to control, to react to the unexpected, and to act coolly and with purpose.

Such characteristics are not universally available although many who have found themselves having to deal with unexpected emergencies have been surprised by their own unforeseen capabilities. All other things being equal, the experienced and well prepared leader will be most likely to be successful in demanding circumstances – but others are undoubtedly able to rise to the challenge.

Technical skills

For a particular session or journey the leader's technical skills should normally include:

- an understanding of the activity to be undertaken, usually demonstrated by an appropriate level of personal experience, involvement and achievement;
- an adequate level of personal proficiency, so as not to be at risk when moving around to assist participants;
- an ability to coach novices in the main techniques of the activity;
- a familiarity with the main hazards likely to be encountered and how these are to be controlled;
- the effect of weather, sea state, water levels and other external factors;
- appropriate equipment and its use;
- knowledge of any grading systems that indicate difficulty or danger;
- rescue and emergency arrangements.

In many cases, prior knowledge of the operating site is desirable but skilled instructors will often have a sufficiently high level of generic expertise to be able to operate safely at new locations.

One would normally expect the leader to communicate enthusiasm for the activity and have background knowledge about its history, structure, key personalities and so on. Instructors can easily get into a mindset that sees activity sessions as never to be repeated, one-off 'tasters' with little connection to the core values of the activity; but it is worth remembering that a small number of those taking part will go on to sustained personal involvement in kayaking, skiing or whatever. In any case, all beginners deserve to have an activity presented in a form that its devotees would recognise as containing the essence of its appeal. Nobody articulated to me the core values of climbing on my first day at Wharncliffe Crags but, and largely because it was presented in a form true to the sport, I knew instinctively that it was about judgement and control, problem-solving, brain and brawn in balance – and was hooked!

Leadership skills

The necessary leadership and group management skills depend strongly on context. Different groups make different demands on leaders. Some who are excellent leaders with a group of enthusiastic adults may struggle to reach the same quality of management with younger and less motivated groups.

Having a number of different hues on the leadership palette, and the knowledge when and how to use them, is a great asset in the instructor because what is demanded also varies with the situation that prevails. A group of nervous, poorly socialised youngsters are unlikely to benefit from a permanently authoritarian leadership style; conversely, when the building is burning down, it is hardly the time for the leader to call everyone together and say: 'Now, I would really like to hear what every person thinks we should do here, so we are going to sit in a circle and give every-one a say… '

A cheerful and enthusiastic instructor is a great asset.

Since we all have preferred styles, a degree of self-knowledge is desirable in order to avoid one approach becoming dominant at the expense of others more suitable. The appropriate style can shift considerably as the entirety of the situation changes. Hersey and Blanchard's theory, Situational Leadership, describes this shifting balance between the leader's directive and supportive roles.

Compulsion or laissez-faire?

The leader is the person most able to manage the participant's interaction with the activity and has to tread a delicate path between acceptance and rejection of the challenge. Rarely will there be a situation where compulsion is desirable. If engaging with challenge is to mean anything, then declining that engagement has got to be a clear option. Some people call this 'challenge by choice' and its importance goes beyond any educational value since the existence of a right of veto by participants appears to be an important factor in determining consent and understanding in the eyes of the law.

Yet this does not mean that the leader should adopt 'take it or leave it' as a regular philosophy; we all know that the rewards of engagement are high and so a certain amount of 'selling' to learners is called for. 'Impel' is a very good word that emerged from the early days of Outward Bound®, a word which seems to capture a level of encouragement and enthusiastic persuasion that stops short of compulsion. Jim Hogan, one of the founding fathers of Outward Bound®, called his book *Impelled into Experiences*, which is hard to better as a catchphrase of adventure education at its best.

One of the most difficult things for the leader, and one that has a powerful effect on the quality of the learning experience, is to pitch the challenge at the right level for each individual. This requires a strong focus on individuals and not simply on the group. John Adair's well proven leadership model exhorts leaders to pay attention to:

- achieving the task;
- building the team;
- developing individuals.

His original theory is called Action-Centred Leadership, which as a central tenet has a belief that it is what the leader *does* rather than what they *are* that matters most. While the greatest leaders may be born, most of us can learn to lead effectively by learning to do what leaders need to do – including, of course, the contents of the three circles (see Chapter 6).

This is good news for aspiring outdoor leaders who, although they may not feel blessed with the attributes of Raold Amundsen or James Cook, can, with focus and experience, develop a high level of leadership skill. The young Amundsen's programme for building his own experience and knowledge of skiing and sledge dogs, sailing and snow, clearly demonstrates a commitment to his own development that was to pay great rewards years later.

Some instructors are driven by routine and always seem to offer the same level of challenge, perhaps voicing the unconvincing argument that it is the taking part that matters more than the success. Better ones impel learners into a bespoke level of adventure that pitches challenge and uncertainty at a level where their ultimate resolution is an attainable but not a guaranteed outcome.

Pastoral care

Most leaders will have to provide some element of pastoral care. This can be particularly important with children on residential experiences where there is a 24-hour need for care, and which can include a huge range of interventions including supportive adult contact, the management of medical needs, intervention in cases of bullying and inappropriate relationships and, very occasionally, dealing appropriately with disclosures of dreadful seriousness. Such issues are of the greatest importance. It is desirable for young people undertaking adventure activities to have access to adults of the same gender as themselves.

It is well to remember that a great many incidents occur in unsupervised or loosely supervised periods. Pupils run down flights of steps when we might prefer them to walk, throw things, get into fights and generally try to push the envelope of their situation. Adolescent males are particularly creative in finding ways to injure themselves in what might be considered innocuous locations. A typical example is the group of 14 year olds who, in their free time after a successful day of closely supervised activities, had a competition to see who could jump onto a hard surface from the greatest height. One lad overtopped all other attempts but, alas, was disqualified by a broken leg.

It is difficult for the person in charge single-handedly to provide general supervision and pastoral care over an extended period. Sometimes responsible but otherwise non-specialist adults can give invaluable help but they will need careful briefing on the parameters and limits of their duties. A common model in outdoor centres is that the centre's instructional staff share pastoral responsibility with visiting teachers. The boundaries and extent of these responsibilities must be clearly defined to avoid ambiguity as to who is responsible for what. 'Mind the gap' indeed.

Shared leadership

Having more than one leader, or a leader supported by an assistant, can enhance the quality of decision-making by allowing a degree of discussion of alternatives and by having more people to spot the first signals of a problem developing. However, it is almost always desirable to have a single person who is in overall control and known by everyone else to have that responsibility. A number of unfortunate accidents have occurred in groups under

This instructor is clearly in charge.

shared leadership when a developing threat has been left unaddressed because each leader has left their concerns unvoiced, thinking that the other person was in charge, or that if there was a problem, the other would have already identified it. Having a clear locus for important decisions may not eliminate this kind of occurrence but it certainly renders it less likely.

Selecting a leader

Having toured some of the key requirements of the ideal leader it is hard to avoid concluding that to lead any activity we need some superhuman individual who can do everything from sailing several times round the world single handed to converting the most deeply negative of adolescents to wild enthusiasm. It is perhaps fortunate that such perfection is extremely rare. When we appoint the leader we are back in the real world and have to aim for the best available match to an extremely wide set of demands.

Selection

The process by which a leader is identified, appointed and deployed can be represented by a largely linear sequence such as:

> Identification of need – Specification of post – Advertising – Selection – Screening – Appointment – Induction – Authorisation – Monitoring of performance – Re-validation.

Some of these stages may be considered unnecessary in a particular situation. Initial selection to a long-term post is likely to focus on the entire breadth of possible responsibility and to then be followed by in-house induction. Screening is intended to confirm general suitability and routine attributes or skills such as being of a suitable age, holding a first-aid certificate, a driving licence, police check and so on.

At some point, authorisation for specific activities must take place activity by activity. Some very able instructors in one activity such as kayaking may not be at all equipped to instruct, say, mountaineering or sailing. Even between activities that seem closely related such as kayaking and open canoeing there may be very important operational differences.

Some organisations choose to train and then assess would-be instructors in all the core activities that might be delivered so that an authorised instructor can do 'everything'. This, for an organisation, is an attractively efficient process but runs the risk of instructors being allowed to scrape through with marginal competence in certain activities so as not to force a withholding of their entire instructor status. My own preference is for a piecemeal approach since this is more likely to give consistent quality of output.

When instructors are recruited as long-term professional employees the normal job selection arrangements usually suffice. The panel should include people able to form an opinion on both technical and leadership issues. When candidates hold National Governing Body (NGB) awards it is important to ensure that the proposed level of activity falls within the remit of the particular award – only some of the awards of the highest level will cover the entire range of an activity.

When selection is undertaken for short-term, freelance or voluntary positions, the importance of the decision remains high, but the resources to assure its accuracy tend to be constrained. If what is being sought is a leader for a single activity then the selecting agency can probably join the linear sequence outlined above at the 'authorisation' stage. However, if the appointment covers a variety of activities and a variety of pastoral responsibilities then it is hard to escape the need to follow the same steps as for long-term instructors.

Authorisation

Authorisation is the process by which we give an instructor or leader our approval as competent to operate in a particular activity. It is a very important process and one that is often ignored, particularly in less formal organisations such as the operation of voluntary groups or clubs. For the process to be convincing we should aim to include the following features:

- Authorisation to operate is given by a single individual of demonstrable competence in the activity, who 'signs off' the would be leader. The opinions of others may be sought but the buck should stop at an identifiable person.

- That a demonstrably competent individual should hold high-level National Governing Body (NGB) awards when these are available for the activity in question, and preferably to a level that would allow them to be recognised as a Technical Adviser.

- Criteria of competence relating to both technical and leadership skills should be used as the basis of the decision on authorisation.

- Any judgement that an individual leader or instructor meets these criteria of competence should be based on evidence.

- Evidence can include demonstrations of knowledge or practical skills, prior or comparable experience, external certification, opinions of colleagues.

- A summary of the evidence used should be recorded.

- The authorisation should be documented, with identification of the date, the person authorised, the person giving the authorisation, the activity and scope of the authorisation, any relevant limitations and the date of any required revalidation.

The documentation assists traceability and supports the position of both authoriser and authorised should the decision of competence be brought into question at a future time.

This ideal process all sounds dauntingly complex but simply to make an unsubstantiated claim that 'all our leaders are extremely competent' is no longer acceptable.

Attendance at training courses is often used as part of the evidence of competence of an instructor but this should not be used as a reliable indication of competence. Would you fly in an aeroplane piloted by someone who had been trained but not assessed? It is perfectly reasonable to regard training courses as relevant and focused experience.

Qualification and certification

At this point it is impossible to avoid stepping into a semantic maze concerning the way that we describe the strongest categories of evidence of competence. Originally a person could be 'qualified', say to lead a canoe journey, by dint of long experience, demonstrated skills and all the other criteria for authorisation listed above.

Some other candidates would be 'certified' by an external body, such as an NGB like the Royal Yachting Association or the Union International des Guides de Montagne, as evidence that their competence has been measured and examined by highly competent specialists. Such certification is particularly valuable to potential employers who may not themselves have the ability to assess competence in a specialist area.

Unfortunately, the two terms appear to have now become synonymous and there is a growing expectation of external qualifications as the benchmark of competence. This devalues the process of authorisation, which, when done thoroughly, is probably the best assurance of all-round competence. It also tends to ignore some of the weaknesses of NGB awards.

Most NGB awards are of very high quality and are, without question, a good demonstration of competence. However, they usually have a dominant technical emphasis which may be disproportionate to the demands of the instructor's role. There often appears to be a steady inflation in the technical demands of such awards.

NGBs have started to pay attention to people-centred leadership skills and the process of judgement but there is much to be done. Few awarding bodies will directly assess in these 'human factor' areas. Some NGBs expressly state that their awards are confined to matters technical and that employers must satisfy themselves on the personal suitability of candidates to lead. It is hard to argue with this as an absolute principle, but the employer may simply be taking someone on for a few days' work and may not be a specialist in the area of qualification. How are they to reach a decision?

Candidates holding NGB awards may have spent several days with a skilled assessor; surely that individual is in a position to form an opinion on matters of style, personality and judgement that might better inform potential employers? Psychometric instruments have given illumination in other areas and, even if confined to training, can at least give potential leaders insights into their preferred styles, their methods of interaction with others and their methods of assimilating and disseminating information.

The importance of human factors is discussed elsewhere but experience tells us that, as precursors of the most serious accidents, deficiencies in technical skills are often much less important than deficiencies in leadership and judgemental skills.

Screening

Some countries now have a legal requirement for those who are to work with young people to have gone through a process of screening which is intended to identify any criminal record relating to offences against young people. In Britain this is done by the Criminal Records Bureau (CRB) in England and Wales and by Disclosure Scotland.

Monitoring

Monitoring the operational performance of leaders is an important part of the assurance of quality and safety. Systems of peer review have been used to great effect but there is a strong argument that managers, and others with supervisory responsibility, should make regular field visits to see leaders working. Since managers are often very busy people it is desirable to give this process of observation a level of priority that will ensure it takes place. Constructive feedback on quality, safety and style of operation should be given to the instructor concerned.

Re-validation

Some NGB awards include a compulsory component of re-validation, others do not. The intention is to ensure that a qualified instructor remains current with recent developments in good practice. Except in very rapidly changing fields, instructors who work regularly in a particular discipline and who are in regular contact with colleagues have a good chance of remaining current and effective. Re-validation should not place an unreasonable burden on such individuals. When leaders operate in isolation, or where they only lead an activity infrequently, there is a greater danger of them being out of touch and re-validation is then desirable. A three-yearly time scale is often used. Keeping employees current is a responsibility of the employer and re-validation is often a professional requirement for the instructor.

Volunteer leaders

Let it be acknowledged in the most emphatic terms that volunteer leaders are vital in giving many people the opportunity to experience adventurous activities and outdoor recreation. Hugely influential youth organisations like the Duke of Edinburgh's Award, the Scouts and the Guides simply could not function without the extensive and wonderful support of volunteer leaders. Many children would have never seen the sunrise or slept under the stars without the commitment of volunteers.

In the adult sector, many clubs and mass participation organisations like the Ramblers' Association have exactly the same dependence on volunteers. When asked why they do it, many of these volunteers explain how 'they want to put something back', often tracing their own involvement back to the enthusiasm of a volunteer during a formative period in their own lives.

So what should be our expectations of such volunteers? What should they expect of the sponsoring organisation and it of them? How should voluntary leaders be selected and authorised?

It is hard to escape the view, unpalatable to some, that our expectations from volunteer leaders are rather similar to those that we have from professionals. This is at its clearest with young people. Will any parent really want their child to go walking along an exposed coastal path, or white water kayaking, or sailing in an estuary, or rock climbing with a leader who does not meet most of the criteria of safety and quality outlined above?

Some differences exist with adults because it is more acceptable for adults to make decisions, preferably informed decisions, about their own safety.

Judgement

Few would dispute that judgement is an important attribute of outdoor leaders. What exactly judgement is and how to identify or develop it are more difficult questions. Further relevant information can be found in Chapter 8.

Staff health and safety

We want instructors to be safe. Employers have a legal duty of care, and it is clear that if an instructor is incapacitated during a session when they have supervisory responsibility, the safety of group members is likely to be, in turn, jeopardised. Chapter 8 has more to say about the instructor's approach to safety but there are additional aspects. Instructors are often working in arduous environments and it is desirable to ensure that working practices minimise the long-term effect of this work – a challenge because instructors are often so passionate about their sports that, on days off, they are to be found taking part in the same activities that they instruct in work time, but at a higher level of intensity.

The AAIAC recently published advice which included this comment to instructors:

> Imagine being unable to go up a hill because your knees are worn out, unable to paddle because of chronic ear problems, unable to sail because of permanent back injury. Some can no longer even contemplate such activities as a result of a serious accident at work. Many instructors who have ended up with these problems could have avoided them with better working practices.

General health and safety issues such as safe lifting can be eclipsed in outdoor sports by more exciting concerns, but they remain important. Lifting a kayak full of water, shifting a sailing dinghy or hoisting someone on the end of a rope are all strenuous and need a suitably ergonomic approach.

Child protection policies, quite rightly, have children at their core, but there is an overlapping need to educate staff into working practices that reduce their exposure to compromising situations or even false accusations. In the relaxed atmosphere of residential outdoor education, staff can be vulnerable and should be aware of simple good practice relating to the personal privacy of students, especially with respect to physical contact and access to sleeping areas and toilet facilities.

When an instructor fits a climbing harness or a buoyancy aid, it is desirable to avoid unnecessary physical contact by instructing the student to do most of the fitting themselves. When direct contact is necessary, such as when a child cannot adequately tighten a buckle, then this should be done in clear view of the rest of the group.

When it is necessary to enter sleeping areas, staff should knock or call before entering and, preferably, should be accompanied by a colleague.

Aggressive behaviour

Aggressive behaviour can readily spring out of the combination of frustration and fatigue that often occurs during challenging activities. Instructors are in the front line when this occurs and can often become the target against which aggression is directed. Some training in how to defuse tense situations is desirable for all staff, but essential for those who habitually work with challenging or volatile individuals and groups.

I heard of a case where an instructor, understandably frustrated by the continuing reluctance of a young adult to turn up to the group's morning meeting, stormed into the torpid youth's dormitory and poured cold water onto him. It will surprise no one to hear that the lad lashed out and the instructor ended up with a broken nose. This instructor's approach was not one calculated to defuse aggression!

Fatigue

Anybody that wants to work a regular nine till five day is not likely to enjoy being an outdoor instructor. The irregularity and variety of the work is part of its appeal – overnight bivouacs, multi-day journeys, dawns and sunsets are all part of the package.

Managers and instructors themselves have a duty to avoid levels of fatigue that might adversely affect judgement and safety. The European Working Time Directive directly addresses this, but even within its operation, demanding periods can occur. Keeping records of hours worked is important but it can also be worthwhile to differentiate between student contact time and other hours. Having undue fatigue in open view as an issue of concern is a way of preventing problems arising.

Participants

Adults and minors

The law differs in its treatment of adults and minors and so must we. What is reasonable for an adult may be extremely unreasonable for a minor. In Britain, those under 18 years of age are regarded as minors. The Adventure Activities (Young Persons' Safety) Act 1995 applies only to that age group. At the time of writing, there is no specific regulation of the same kind that is applicable to provision targeted at adults, although the Health and Safety at Work Act 1974 applies as it does to most other enterprises.

Instructors who work with youngsters often develop a highly effective rapport which seems to be part parent, part teacher and part wild elder sibling. Those who primarily work with adults need a different style and different means of communication.

Adults may be adept at absorbing information from written sources or formal briefing; with children it can be more effective to allow them to discover key facts, perhaps from some kind of clue search.

A danger signal is an organisation working with any kind of unfamiliar client group. The young person's centre that has a one-off adult programme can be caught out by the different demands made by that age group.

Medical screening

Medical screening helps us to learn more about exactly who we are dealing with and how we can best take care of their safety and development. In almost all cases it is desirable for the leader to be aware of any illnesses, medical conditions or disabilities that might directly affect the safety of the participant or others. In effect, we are doing a risk assessment with respect to matters concerning health and physiology. The conditions that combine frequency of occurrence with potential severity include:

- asthma;
- allergy;
- epilepsy;
- diabetes;
- heart disease.

Firstly we have to ask would-be participants, or for minors their parent or guardian, to indicate if these conditions exist, determine the severity and effect of the condition and then decide:

- Does attendance require modifications to programme content or supervision ratios?
- Is the condition a bar to participation?
- Are special arrangements necessary for medication or other management?
- What information should we communicate to staff or other group members?

Expert opinion may be necessary. The UK Disability Discrimination Act 1995 makes it illegal for providers of services to discriminate against those with disabilities. Advocates of outdoor activities often enthusiastically embrace a policy of open access to activities regardless of physical capability. This is laudable but the need to make consequent adjustments to the arrangements for risk management should follow automatically and is implied in the Act.

A person who has epilepsy with fairly frequent seizures can take part in many adventure activities but those involving height or water may need special arrangements in the form of equipment (for example, wearing a lifejacket on water at all times) or staffing, such as a close supervisory ratio. A child with diabetes may need considerable support to ensure that their dosage of insulin matches the unusual physical and emotional demands of an outdoor course and so on. A case by case approach is desirable in order to keep the individual, not the disability, in view. If we cannot always simply say 'Yes' we should try hard to be able to say 'Yes – but with some modifications to our standard practices'.

All medical information should be managed in a way that respects an individual's right to confidentiality and privacy.

Child protection

This is the term used to describe arrangements which exist to raise the level of protection afforded to children with respect to:

- bullying;
- disclosures;
- physical assault;
- sexual assault.

The arrangements will normally involve training staff in the recognition of warning signs and the application of the child protection policy, and will identify individuals and external agencies as the contact in the event of a concern or an occurrence of one of the above.

Training is vital because the 'common-sense' approach often contains many pitfalls.

It should be recognised that the particular informality of outdoor activities may make them an attractive field of operation for the very occasional individual with suspect motives.

Although, with good reason, much of this section is concerned with children's welfare, there is also a need to recognise the rights and needs of adults. Bullying is not confined to those of school age.

Contribution to safety

Participants are an invaluable resource for managing risks, whose ability to contribute can be overlooked. They can contribute by:

- checking, by a 'buddy system', the fitting and use of safety equipment;
- ensuring that they understand all instructions;
- letting the leader know if they are anxious or uncertain;
- letting the leader know of anyone in difficulties.

A more formal system might invite participants to report unsafe occurrences in a similar way to that which we expect from staff. This brings many extra eyes to the process and aids a raising of safety awareness.

Briefing

It is desirable for participants to be briefed at the start of a programme. This also gives the provider a further opportunity to learn about participants. Not everyone needs the same information but some of the information that that has a safety content might include:

- welcome and introductions;
- our approach to safety – how you can contribute;
- house procedures and rules;
- access to sleeping areas;
- unsupervised use of activities and apparatus;
- fire arrangements;
- emergency contact;
- night duty and contact;
- right of veto on participation
- local traffic hazards;
- any changes to the confidential medical information supplied;
- policy on drugs, tobacco and alcohol;
- swimming ability.

Briefing for individual activity sessions should address the central safety issues. As an example, action in the event of a capsize is a necessary part of briefing for most sessions in kayaks, canoes and dinghies. However, as long as the core safety information has been covered, a skilled instructor may decide that the adventure and educational impact of a session will be enhanced by not over-briefing. Inexperienced instructors tend to transmit too much information. The learner rock climber, itching to get on the rock, does not need to be told every detail of how ropes are manufactured and tested before being allowed to leave the ground.

Chapter summary

- Staff are the key influence on safety.
- Outdoor leaders usually need to combine both leadership and technical skills.
- Leadership skills are about the interaction with participants.
- Technical skills are about the interaction with the activity.
- Effective leaders have learnt to use different styles of leadership in different contexts.
- Authorisation is the important process by which a leader is judged to have the experience, skills and attributes to take charge of a party in a particular session.
- Competence can be demonstrated by the holding of appropriate certification but also by other means drawing on prior experience and in-house vetting.
- Knowledge about a participant's medical condition, fitness and expectations helps providers to provide an appropriate level of care.
- Certain clients will require modified levels of care in order to undertake an activity.

Chapter 4

Culture – the learning organisation

There are a great many things that can go wrong with adventure activities. Because we are dealing with highly unpredictable elements, such as people and the great outdoors, it can be very difficult to know where problems might emerge and where best we should focus our attention. Nobody welcomes things going wrong, but the silver lining in that particular cloud is the fact that every adverse occurrence can be a valuable source of information.

Experiential learning – learning by doing – is at the heart of adventure education, but every trainer who runs soft skill review sessions will know that it can be difficult for individuals to be open and honest about their own mistakes or problems and to see the same mistakes as a source of valuable learning. At an organisational level the same reluctance can hinder effective risk management. We need to work hard to establish a culture where this will happen.

An effective safety culture

Some words that we might apply to a safety culture that is likely to be effective in learning from experience are:

- prominent
- specific
- universally owned
- responsive
- honest
- open
- non-punitive
- learning
- ambitious
- optimistic.

Prominent

Risk management should be a function that is in prominent view during normal day-to-day operation and not one which is only wheeled out when there is a problem. If we only consult the map when lost we are unlikely to have developed the skills to make good use of it at that time.

The standing of the function is greatly enhanced if senior staff are seen to take an interest in its routine operation and not only when a crisis occurs. Even managers who do not have specialist skills should ask questions and seek clarification about field operation.

The induction of new staff should emphasise the importance of risk management and outline their own contribution.

Adventure and challenge – in a few seaside boulders. An effective safety culture ensures that activities like this can take place within acceptable boundaries.

Specific

People readily assume that 'safety' is something so indisputably good that we all mean the same thing by it and all try to achieve it in the same way. This is far from being true and it is important for those involved to be clear about what is expected.

The level of tolerable risk is a topic that illuminates this. Mountaineers who go into the so called 'death zone' on the highest mountains, engaging with frostbite and storms, sometimes pose the question 'What would you be willing to suffer in order to climb the most famously challenging mountain in the world? A blister? A lost fingernail? A lost finger? A lost foot? Loss of your life?' The answer is not without practical importance in helping the climber to decide when to turn back or to go on. What is certain is that you will get widely varying answers to the question – because we all have different settings on our risk thermostats (see Chapter 2).

Similarly, although likely to be in less extreme situations, outdoor leaders and outdoor adventure providers must decide what their normal tolerance is of the risk to which their clients are exposed. Is it your goal to have no accidental injuries? If so you are setting a very high standard that will be hard to attain.

Or is your goal no fatal or disabling injuries? This is perhaps more realistic but a line must still be drawn. Would you really regard a broken leg as representing a tolerable level of injury? Would your clients understand this?

So, it is worthwhile to be specific about our goals and the same applies to our performance. Ideally we will be able to use measurable criteria and the analysis of incident data described in Chapter 13 will provide this, at least to larger organisations. Even if we are unable to provide numerical data (of which trends are the most valuable aspect) we can at least iden-tify the areas of strength and the areas of concern in a way that informs future operation. 'Since improving the flow of information to leaders we seem to have had some very success-ful and well run unaccompanied expeditions but there is still a problem with undeclared asthma cases that we need to look at' might be an example.

Open and universally owned

It is not difficult to see that everyone has an influence on their own safety. What is less immediately clear is that everyone has an influence on the safety of many others. Bertie Everard once described it to me as an 'unlimited personal responsibility for safety'. The safety of participants in an outdoor programme are certainly dependent on the contribu-tions of many others:

- administrators – accurate and appropriate medical screening;
- maintenance staff – quality maintenance of facilities and equipment;
- caterers – wholesome food;
- managers – appropriate systems, supervision and resources;
- drivers – safe travel;
- instructors – safe activity provision;
- fellow students – support and encouragement.

It is a mistake to behave as though risk management is confined to managers and instruc-tors. Recruiting the rest of the team to contribute not just to their immediate job role but also to the wider operation is very worthwhile. Maintenance staff spot unauthorised use of an activity and intervene, catering staff pick up on the emergence of bullying, drivers hear some suspicious comments about illegal substances and so on.

When there is information to report back on safety performance or changes to key systems it is helpful to include everybody.

Responsive

Nothing kills a risk management system as effectively as unresponsiveness. Somebody takes the trouble to bring a safety concern to the boss's attention and then absolutely nothing happens. Every concern raised does not necessarily warrant action but the reporter does deserve to be informed about the decisions made, especially if this is one to take no action. Most people are reasonable if the grounds for action (or inaction) are explained but they hate to be ignored.

Honest

We are not engaged in a PR exercise. Sometimes, difficult and painful truths must be addressed if we are going to climb the ladder to where we want to be, and it is difficult to do this if we hide behind euphemisms and half truths. Nothing would make me more suspicious than an instructor who claimed never to have had any anxious moments when leading, or a provider who maintains that they have had no accidents.

Non-punitive

If we want to learn from things that go wrong and encourage an open safety culture we cannot expect to punish every minor transgression. This is not to ignore problems that occur, but to take a longer view and a more mature position on how to change the behaviour of people and organisations.

When an error has been made managers should welcome reports that reach them, and be willing to shoulder blame if there is any possible component of organisational responsibility. Many leaders have got into difficulties because they have found themselves in a situation for which they have not been trained or prepared.

When a leader has been involved in some kind of accident or other undesirable occurrence, they will need the support and encouragement of colleagues, not a flaying for some supposed error.

Disciplinary measures are best kept for extreme cases, such as when someone wilfully ignores advice and direct instructions on good practice, or deliberately behaves in a way that jeopardises their own safety or that of others.

Learning

If we don't learn from what goes wrong, in risk management as in life, we are in deep trouble. Much of this book is concerned with enhancing this learning and it is the central theme of Chapter 16.

Ambitious

Effecting culture change is a slow process and this can be especially true of voluntary organisations. We need to take the long view but need also to lift our spirits on the journey by having a destination in sight. Most operators will find that there is a residual level of incidents that remains intractable, but persistence really will pay dividends in the end. And that is where the optimism comes in.

Optimistic

Optimism is a reflection of an organisation with self-belief: 'We may not have anticipated every unfortunate occurrence but we are confident that our superb staff will deal with the unexpected in an exemplary manner.'

Establishing a safety culture

Safety is usually an accepted value in outdoor organisations, but this accepted value is often given lip service rather than a genuine operational priority. Managers say 'safety is paramount' but there may be little evidence of this in what they do, or how their budget priorities are set, or how staff are deployed. However, the wide acceptance of the value of safety gives an essential platform for further development; radical change towards completely fresh values is rarely necessary. Safety issues need to be kept in view and managers need to set the tone of safety as a core value and a key behaviour. A constant drip feed is likely to be more effective than the very occasional spectacular. Keep the issues and information prominent and time will do the rest.

Any scale of operation, from sole traders to large multi-site operations, can, and at regular occasions should, pose the questions:

- Have there been any recent incidents of note?
- Are there any current concerns for the safety of participants, staff and others?
- Have there been any notable recent incidents?

These can be included in staff meetings, as a routine agenda item for management committees or as topics of informal discussion.

Having regular updates on safety issues and safety performance pays dividends and the case studies and digests described in Chapter 13 help to get the lessons across. Many NGBs and activity magazines disseminate safety information and their guidance can be put on display, filed in a 'Read' file or sent to staff as a circular e-mail.

The process is never simple but is without doubt more straightforward for groups that work together or regularly meet. Widely distributed organisations, such as some of the voluntary youth organisations where many individuals each plough their own furrow, need to work hard to share good practice and to bring people together for safety updates or focused discussion.

Chapter summary

- Adverse incidents may not be welcomed but are an opportunity to learn valuable lessons for future operation.

- This is most likely to happen if the organisation has a culture of safety.

- Safety culture should be prominent, specific, universally owned, responsive, honest and open.

- Useful questions are:

    - Have there been any recent incidents of note?
    - Are there any current concerns for the safety of participants and staff?
    - Have there been any notable recent incidents?

Chapter 5

Systems – making it all work

Systems need to reflect and complement the way your organisation operates. A sole provider of outdoor services may be able manage with a bare minimum of systems and should, at least, be confident that internal communications will operate smoothly. However, even a sole operator will suffer from having a limited span concerning the number of things to which she or he can give attention at the same time; a few basic systems can allow some of the thinking and planning to be done in advance and allow closer attention to be given to the immediate priorities of the moment, in the confident knowledge that the backup systems are already thought through and in place.

A large organisation with many staff and many clients will inevitably need more highly refined systems and controls. It is important here to ensure that systems actually achieve what they are assumed to achieve, and are not simply an apparently well organised facade lying over a core of disorganised chaos. A yawning trap for managers is to assume that because a system has been written down, everyone is adhering to its recommendations. Any system or policy needs to installed and embedded by a conscious effort of communication and training.

It can be particularly difficult for large organisations to operate systems that are able to deal successfully with small facets of the enterprise – it is like asking an elephant to pick daisies. A few high-profile outdoor tragedies have illuminated the fact that communications and the effective exercise of control and flow of guidance between an education authority, which may have hundreds of schools under its aegis, and individual schools, or worse, individual teachers providing outdoor education in the field, have been unreliable. Substantial delegation of control and guidance is desirable, but this delegation can only occur successfully if the necessary expertise exists close to the point of delivery of the outdoor experiences.

After several such serious accidents in Britain, government guidance to schools introduced Educational Visit Coordinators (EVCs) into schools to be involved in the planning and management of educational visits led by school staff. The visits would include adventure activities, outdoor education and other out-of-school learning. EVCs represent a delegation of the supervisory and screening function to the level of individual schools. EVCs are not necessarily outdoor specialists but they will have undergone training and will understand:

- the processes of screening, approval and parental permission;
- when and where to seek particular advice from technical specialists and others.

The EVC's responsibilities include:

- ensuring that educational visits meet the employer's requirements including those of risk assessment;
- supporting the head and school governors with approval and other decisions;
- assigning competent people to lead and supervise a visit;
- assessing the competence and suitability of leaders and other adults proposed for a visit;
- organising the training of leaders and other adults going on a visit;
- ensuring the provision of necessary training and induction for leaders;
- providing full details of the visit beforehand so that parents can consent or refuse consent on a fully informed basis;
- organising the emergency arrangements and ensuring there is an emergency contact for each visit;
- keeping records of individual visits including reports of accidents and 'near-accidents' ('near misses');
- reviewing systems and, from time to time, monitoring practice.

These duties represent some of the main systems that should be in place when an out-of-school visit is planned.

So what is a system?

Within the context of outdoor risk management a system is something that is intended to help us to manage a specified area of concern. It often involves:

- a standardisation of operation between certain limits;
- a flow of information;
- someone monitoring that information;
- a method for responding to that information with advice or action.

Thus a 'late back system' might be introduced by an outdoor centre, so that if a group is late back from an activity, somebody will notice this and react accordingly. Such a system is particularly important when the scale of operation is such that no single individual can be expected to track the progress and status of every group. It is also a way of reducing the chance of an overdue group falling below the radar, something that easily happens when staff go home after normal office hours and night-duty staff take over.

The system might be designed and operate like this:

- Every group outlines their plans and states an expected time back at the morning meeting.

- This is displayed on a whiteboard which might show an entry such as:

  7/8/2006 Jane Pearson. Group of 8. Pen y Pass – Miners' Track – Pen y Pass. Own vehicle. Due back 16:30.

- Instructors are expected to sign the board to indicate when they and their group are safely back at base.

- By 17:00 the group are not back. This does not trigger any particular concern but is noted by the duty manager.

- Just before handing over to night duty staff at 17:30 the duty manager attempts to phone Jane Pearson on her mobile telephone (the DM has contact numbers for all instructors) but gets no response. He knows that Jane is a very capable instructor and is also aware that although some of her group are pretty slow walkers they are very persistent.

- The night-duty instructor arrives for the handover. 'Sarah, everyone else is safe back but we haven't heard from Jane's group yet. Weather's OK so I am not too concerned but can you get the kitchen to save dinner for them and give me a call if they still haven't showed up by six thirty?'

- At 18:15 Jane calls in as soon as she has a phone signal. 'We had an excellent day. Everything's fine – simply a slow group. We're back at the van now.'

Instructors sometimes feel that a system like this is a small outburst of the 'nanny state' but the centre director is glad to have had it since its introduction a few years ago following an embarrassing incident. Everybody had failed to register that a group were seriously overdue. They were facing growing difficulties dealing with rising water levels yet nobody else was aware of this until somebody watching TV in the staff room happened to say, 'Has anybody seen Jason this evening? Are they back from the river yet?' Fortunately the team of instructors arrived in time to solve the problem before things got serious – but it had been a close call.

The problem that had led to the new late back arrangements had in turn been picked up by another system which regularly brings the instructor team together to identify any current concerns about safety – and to react accordingly. The system is introduced to new staff during their induction but is also driven and supported by senior staff being seen to take an interest in its application and in the information it generates.

This is a system that works well for this particular centre and its style of operation. If you are running a mountain biking business as the manager and sole instructor, it is a good idea for someone else to know when you plan to return, and to be ready to react if you don't, but you hardly need a whiteboard.

By contrast, if you are in charge of the summer camp for a provider running eighty groups in parallel, you are probably going to need a logistical specialist and a good computer program to manage the daily coming and going of so many groups.

Pitfalls

When anyone devises a system they tend to be blind to its faults. Constructing the system is often the easy part, but you have to recognise that the process does not stop there. The system is only likely to work if:

- people know what the system is expected to do;
- they know what they have to do;
- they see the value of the process or, even better, it makes their own job safer or easier;
- they see it working effectively.

Some things operate perfectly well with an unstructured flexible approach so it might be best to leave well enough alone. The computer program to randomly generate the sandwich menu may be just a step too far!

Systems do not always have to be written down if everyone who will be involved genuinely knows what to do, but remember that new recruits and visitors may benefit from a written summary. It is normally a good idea to keep written guidance to brief notes rather than an extended philosophical essay.

What systems do we need?

In order to do almost anything, your body relies on systems for respiration, digestion, planning, movement, repair, heating, cooling and countless other functions. Poetry and mathematics may be among the highest expressions of our humanity, but poets and mathematicians need the same basic support functions as the rest of us if their creative endeavours are not to come to a very sudden stop.

In the same way, if we aim to provide inspiring outdoor education our creative, life-enhancing endeavours will come to little if the correct support systems are not in place to inform, control and enhance field activities.

There has to be some proportionality here. Not all systems apply with the same necessity to all enterprises since they must be influenced by scale and style of operation, and some are intrinsically more important or influential than others. Some organisations will have a restricted sphere of operation that will avoid the necessity of certain systems – or will it?

If you are a peripatetic outdoor activities worker without fixed facilities you may escape the need for systems concerning facilities and services, but as soon as you decide to rent a residential facility for a weekend you are likely to come face to face with the need for fire precautions and evacuation systems, food hygiene and electrical safety. It is easy to make the false assumption that the risks may be very small when you are making a once-only visit to a facility.

And what if the suspension points fail . . . ? How many systems apply here?

If you use a reputable and regulated provider this may not present undue difficulties beyond the need for familiarisation and briefing because they will have already addressed the issues of concern. On the more adventurous kind of journey, the leader's control over the quality of what is provided can be very limited. A facility may not meet desirable standards but there may be absolutely no alternative if you have arrived in the middle of nowhere, tired, cold and weary.

In August 1998 a fire destroyed the three-storey aluminium Priut II Hut at 13,800' on Mount Elbrus (18,481') in the Caucasus mountains of Russia when a number of groups were in residence. This is usually regarded as the highest summit in Europe, and is very popular with guided parties so the hut was often overcrowded. Every single drop of water had to be melted from snow and the fierce winds outside meant that many visitors were tempted to operate stoves in cramped, unsuitable conditions.

The fire was thought to have started as a result of an out of control liquid fuel stove. A bystander who stepped in to dowse the flames with what he incorrectly thought was a container of water, actually poured more fuel onto the flames! Fortunately, the fire broke out during daylight hours and most of those staying there were able to get out – but some serious injuries occurred.

Before this incident, who would have thought of routinely going through a fire evacuation briefing with a group or checking escape routes (of which there were very few)? Such preparation could, in the event, have been of vital importance. The final irony is that the Priut I hut also stood on the same restricted site – and was also destroyed by fire.

The next section gives an overview of some of the core systems that you might consider for your own operation.

Core systems

Risk management has an impact on a great many functions and practice in each of them in turn influences the quality of risk management. The main functions of most outdoor operations would include some or all of the following:

Staff	Activities	Participants	Plant and equipment
Transportation services	Facilities and response	Emergency	Review and audit
Communication	Information	Legal	Administration

Of course, although these sit comfortably in separate boxes, the reality is that there is a degree of overlap and interaction between functions which, on the face of it, appear separate. Just as in the human body an injured knee can manifest itself in a painful neck so a defect in the transportation function can impact upon staff safety, or on the quality of emergency response, or the smooth and safe provision of activities.

When the rare and serious charge of corporate manslaughter is brought it requires there to have been a 'controlling mind' in the operation, one that pulls together these separate functions into an integrated and effective whole. The identification of the importance of this controlling influence makes it clear that ensuring this synergy and interconnection between all functions is one of the key roles of management.

Systems are the levers of control and information flow that allow this to happen and each main operating function will have its own tree of subsystems. Some systems impact upon several different functions; for instance, the recruitment of staff has a big influence on quality and safety but is also a personnel function that is controlled by employment law or equal opportunities legislation. Recruitment of a new staff member may need to trigger legal screening or the issue of appropriate equipment and so on.

Below is a tour of some of the key systems outlining some of the key points to consider.

Staff

- Recruitment
- Induction
- Training
- Authorisation
- Monitoring
- Protection
- Legal screening
- Equipment issue or specification.

These will undoubtedly include some of the most important and influential systems in any operation. Training and authorisation of staff would be at the top of my list for most operations. See Chapter 3 for more.

Activities

- Generic risk assessment
- Site-specific risk assessment
- Approval of new activities and new locations
- Staffing ratios
- Safety rules
- Qualification requirements
- Site access
- Listing of sites
- Interaction with NGBs
- Equal opportunity access
- Equipment
- Maps, charts, guidebooks
- Weather forecasts
- Critical safety equipment
- Use of subcontractors
- Accessing current information
- Incident reporting.

Activity is central to what we do in outdoor education and this is true whether we use it as a catalyst to personal development, a mirror to group behaviour or the raw material of performance coaching. Of these systems the two levels of risk assessment are likely to be of critical importance but so will many others such as staffing ratios, qualification levels and the specification and control of critical safety equipment. The latter refers to items such as lifejackets, climbing harnesses and ropes, where failure in use can have fatal consequences. Other equipment is very important, but a leaking waterproof does not have the instantly serious effect of a failed harness.

'Rules are for fools'. Paul Petzoldt, who is one of the founding fathers of adventure education in the United States, is said to have made the remark, which I take to be one questioning the trust we put into rules and procedures. Documenting good practice or specifying rules of operation may be desirable, helpful even, for the novice leader but are likely to be a feeble imitation of the far-ranging skills of the experienced and practised leader.

Participants

- Medical screening
- Child protection
- Confidential information
- Parental consent
- Pastoral care
- Contact information and arrangements
- Preparation
- Equipment issue and return
- Insurance
- Travel
- Core briefing
- Incident reporting.

We have a legal and a moral duty of care towards those in our charge. These systems help us to discharge that responsibility successfully.

Medical screening is an important safeguard in ensuring that those responsible for a participant's safety know if there are any significant medical issues such as diabetes, asthma, heart disease, epilepsy, allergy, recent injury or infectious diseases. If operated with imagination and a positive approach the system can also help us to say 'yes' to people who may feel that they would be excluded from certain activities, even if this is a 'yes' qualified by certain constraints.

It requires accurate administration to ensure that instructors and others know what they need to know from medical declarations without jeopardising the right to confidentiality of participants.

Plant and equipment

- Specification
- Inspection
- Maintenance
- Compliance with regulations
- Fire certification
- Electrical safety
- Building safety
- Fire safety and evacuation
- Hazardous equipment
- Critical equipment log.

Transportation

- Specification
- Inspection
- Maintenance
- Compliance with regulations
- Carrying of material and equipment
- Use of trailers
- Training of drivers
- Authorisation of drivers
- First-aid kits
- Dealing with adverse weather
- Insurance
- Accident procedure.

Although activities such as canoeing and climbing look spectacular and dangerously 'on the edge', the painful fact is that the most dangerous thing on many outdoor programmes is travelling to and from the place where the activities are to take place. It is almost unheard of for even the most severe rock climbing accident to involve more than a handful of people but minibus and coach accidents can involve many, many more.

Our duty is clear and these systems are aimed at giving us confidence that we are meeting the highest standards for the vehicles that we use and for the way in which they are driven.

Facilities and services

- Food hygiene
- Personal hygiene
- Domestic hygiene
- Nutrition levels
- Dealing with food allergies
- Special diets.

These things are not as glamorous as shooting rapids or wriggling through caves, and although we may take them for granted, they have a big influence on quality and safety. Poor hygiene can readily generate large-scale problems in residential facilities and can easily break out in situations where it is difficult to operate to high standards of hygiene, such as when camping or sailing on a yacht.

I once worked at a big outdoor centre that seemed to get regular outbreaks of what might be politely called gastro-intestinal episodes. These were regarded as 'just one of those things' but someone noticed that the timings of these outbursts tended to follow groups returning from camping expeditions. As an experiment, all of the camping utensils were put through the commercial dishwasher before they were issued afresh and lo and behold – no more problems!

Emergency response

- Emergency plan
- Contact details
- Medical care
- Contact with rescue agencies
- First-aid equipment and training
- Accident investigation

- Rescue equipment
- Rescue training
- Emergency simulation.

See Chapter 11

Review and audit

- Internal review
- External review
- Safety days

See Chapter 12.

Communication of safety information

- Staff
- Participants
- Visitors
- Parents
- Colleagues
- Field communication.

One area that has often caused problems is the flow of safety-related information to and from instructors in activity centres or teachers on out-of-school activities.

A school group starting an activity in a flooded river was unaware that a parallel group from the same school had just had a close escape from rapidly rising water levels. No system was in place to communicate the near miss or to raise the alarm but, even more fundamentally, there had been no risk assessment that recognised the possibility of exceptionally high water levels and the need sometimes to abort the activity. Two pupils drowned.

Information

- Incident reporting
- Incident recording

- Incident analysis
- Lessons learned

See Chapter 13 for more.

Legal

- Compliance with inspections
- Required certification
- Fire certification
- Maintenance of proper records
- Safety at Work Regulations

See Chapter 14

Administration

- Daily diary
- Course programme
- Participant lists
- Staff lists
- Staff files
- Copies of authorisation certificates
- Contact details.

Chapter summary

- Systems need to reflect and complement the way your organisation operates.
- Large organisations often have difficulty with local management in detail – EVCs are a response to this in the education sector.
- Core systems might typically influence the operation of:
  - staff
  - activities

 – participants
 – plant and equipment
 – transportation
 – facilities and services
 – emergency response
 – review and audit
 – communication
 – information
 – legal matters
 – administration.

Chapter 6

Risk assessment

Risk assessment can be a highly effective process for the identification and management of risk. The term features prominently in safety legislation and in advice given by the UK Health and Safety Executive (HSE) in various publications such as *Five Steps to Risk Assessment* and the equivalent advice to adventure activity centres. There is a legal requirement for any enterprise with more than five employees to record the findings of risk assessments and an expectation that smaller operations will aspire to the same standards. The process is normally outlined by the following steps:

- Look for hazards.

- Decide who might be harmed and how.

- Evaluate the risks and decide whether existing precautions are adequate or more should be done.

- Record your findings.

- Review your assessment from time to time and revise if necessary.

Identifying hazards alone is insufficient; there must be some decision made about whether the exposure to that hazard represents a tolerable risk, and, if it does not, control measures – some means of eliminating or mitigating the hazard – must be introduced. The risk assessment should be a process that informs, and continues to inform, good practice, not a product that sits in a filing cabinet.

Unfortunately, in many hands, far from being a powerful tool for improvement, compliance with the regulations ends up being focused only on the paperwork and fails to have much effect on operational practice. In such situations the often heard criticism of risk assessment as a meaningless, bureaucratic paper chase may have some justification.

The greatest attention should be given to hazards that present a threat to life and all reasonable attempts should be made to reduce these to a very low level of risk by eliminating the hazard, using control measures or by modifying or discontinuing the activity.

The hierarchy of risk assessment

As accomplished leaders and voyagers, there is no doubt that both Odysseus and Christopher Columbus were adept at completing risk assessments, even though they would not have been familiar with present terminology. Risk assessments are not a *de novo* invention but, rather, codify what has long been recognised as good practice.

A hierarchy of risk assessments exists, each reflecting a progressively narrower focus:

- generic;
- site specific;
- daily or sessional;
- continuous or dynamic.

Generic risk assessments

A generic risk assessment (GRA) considers the risks that can usually be expected to be present whenever a particular activity is provided. Thus falls during rock climbing and drowning during kayaking are obvious and ever present hazards that would apply whenever the activities occur and so these hazards, together with appropriate control measures, would be listed, among others, in the GRA for each activity.

Less obvious and less serious generic hazards would feature in the respective GRAs. Examples for each of these activities would be the occurrence of rope burns during climbing and fingers being trapped between two boats when kayaking. The simplest format is a three-column model listing:

- Hazard
- Who might be harmed?
- Control measures

with an optional fourth column for Comment.

So, for the examples given, part of each GRA might look like this:

KAYAKING: GENERIC RISK ASSESSMENT (extract)

Hazard	Who might be harmed?	Control measures
Drowning	All	Staff and participants wear well fitting buoyancy **at all times when afloat.**
Trapped fingers	All	Briefing. Care when coming alongside other boats.

ROCK-CLIMBING: GENERIC RISK ASSESSMENT (extract)

Hazard	Who might be harmed?	Control measures
Rope burn	Participants	Control of lowering speed or use of gloves.
Instructor falls	Instructor	Instructor must be secured to an anchor when working within 1.5 metres of any crag edge or steep ground leading to edge.
Participant falls	Participant	On belay when higher than 1.5 metres from ground. Effective spotting and supervision when bouldering.

(Spotting is a means of providing some additional security to someone operating a short way above the ground by having one or more colleagues positioned in close proximity, hands outstretched and ready to intercept or moderate any fall. If done badly it provides only an illusion of security.)

In the second example, the fall hazard is of a different nature for instructors and participants and so a separate listing is used. Those who might be harmed in adventure activities tend to be the participants and/or the instructors, but can also include passers-by, as might be the case if, during a climbing session, a loosened rock fell on to a frequented footpath beneath.

It will be noticed that this simple format does not directly comment on the different severity and frequencies that apply to the various hazards. It is possible to use a more detailed format that reflects this, but my own preference is to use the simplest form of GRA as a clear and simple summary of the primary areas for attention. There can be value in highlighting any items that represent major hazards to life.

Here is an example of applying a numerical scale to both severity and frequency of exposure with an additional comment column:

A Hazards are rated for **severity:**

Rated 1 : serious injury unlikely

Rated 2 : serious injury possible

Rated 3 : serious injury likely

B Likely **frequency of exposure** to hazard is estimated:

Rated 1 : infrequent exposure to hazard

Rated 2 : regular exposure to hazard

Rated 3 : frequent exposure to hazard

Multiplying the two ratings together gives a crude measure of the level risk as the capacity to cause harm:

ROCK CLIMBING: GENERIC RISK ASSESSMENT (extract)

Hazard	Severity	Frequency of exposure	Risk assessment	Control measures	Notes
	A	**B**	**A × B**		
Rope burn	1	2	2	Control of lowering speed or use of gloves.	The greater hazard lies with release of a control rope as a result of the burn.
Instructor falls	3	3	9	Instructor must be secured to an anchor when working within 1.5 metres of any crag edge or on any steep ground where a fall could have serious consequences.	This requires constant attention to avoid complacency.
Participant falls	3	3	9	Climbers must be on belay when higher than 1.5 metres from ground. Effective spotting and supervision when bouldering.	

Clear thinking about risk management can be obscured when there is a suggestion that an algorithm like this can make better operational decisions than an experienced practitioner – it cannot. In addition, there are semantic difficulties about what exactly is meant in this context by the terms 'frequency' and 'severity' that still make it essential for the assessment to be made by such an individual, who is probably sufficiently competent to have little need of the numbers. However, the chosen format should be one that works for the people and the organisation that will be using it. One size does not necessarily fit all.

Figure 6.1 provides an example of a complete GRA. Note that it includes a space to identify who completed the assessment, the date of completion and the date for planned review.

MOUNTAIN BIKING: GENERIC RISK ASSESSMENT

This assessment undertaken by: Jane Brown   Date: August 05

To be reviewed by August 07

Hazard	Who might be harmed?	Control measures
Strain injury	Participants	Warm up and mobilise joints before activity.
Traffic	All	Briefing, supervision. Use of experienced front and back markers. Avoid busy roads.

Hazard	Who might be harmed?	Control measures
Collision	Participants Instructors Passers-by	Briefing, supervision. Control of speed. One at a time on narrow sections.
Falls	All	Avoid exposed sections. Dismount as necessary.
Impact injuries	All	Protective clothing and helmets.
Clothing in chain	Participants	Avoid flapping trousers.
Hypothermia	Participants	Close supervision. Ensure access to shelter and warm clothes. Staff carry spares. Activity may be aborted in adverse conditions.
Eye injuries	All	Wear eye protection.
Equipment failure	All	Careful checks of brakes, bar ends, saddles, drive train, tyres. Instructor to carry tools and spares.

Figure 6.1 Example of a GRA for mountain biking

Site-specific risk assessment

The next level of risk assessment in the hierarchy is the site-specific risk assessment (SSRA). This resembles the GRA but is focused on a particular activity at a particular location. It is likely to incorporate the findings of the GRA together with hazards present at that site but absent from some or all others.

Most leaders and instructors will have a reasonable familiarity with the generic hazards of a sport or activity but they may not readily recognise important additional hazards at

an unfamiliar location. Every climbing instructor will surely know about the hazards of falls but may not realise that the newly chosen crag has an area of unusually loose rock or may also be subject to hazards as diverse as a poisonous giant hogweed plant or bottles thrown from the clifftop by tourists.

Often, these 'new' hazards are to be found on the approach or in the surroundings of the activity site. One may be walking across innocuous moorland to the start of a coastal traverse but a disused mineshaft on the walking approach may be the day's most important hazard.

A trust fall – an activity with some important intrinsic risks. An SSRA would have suggested at least the use of helmets and a site with a softer landing.

The site-specific risk assessment is a powerful tool if it is completed by an experienced practitioner and its findings appropriately disseminated. Once the SSRA has been done it is normal good practice to summarise its findings as a written record. This aids a future review of the findings and recommendations but also, and most importantly, it allows the written risk assessment to be used as an aid to the selection, briefing and training of supervisory staff. I would expect all staff in charge of a particular session to be familiar with the findings and recommendations of the SSRA. It may also be of value to participants and visiting teachers.

Risk assessments are not solely confined to the adventure activities themselves. Figure 6.2 shows part of the SSRA for a residential facility at an adventure centre in North Yorkshire:

VENUE	Centre Grounds
HAZARDS	**CONTROL MEASURES**
Holes in tarmac and broken paving slabs	Cordoned off and replaced/repaired as soon as possible
Wild life area/pond	Warning signs and fence around pond and wild life area
Trees/hedges	Branches at eye height regularly inspected and pruned by grounds staff
	Regular inspection to ascertain health of trees. Diseased trees felled by ground staff
	Trees overhanging paths and driveways pruned or felled by ground staff
	Cordon off areas when necessary
Ropes course	Access restricted to supervised groups and fenced off with warning signs
Vehicles	Students warned on arrival
	Speed restriction signs on the road
Visitors	Visitors must sign in at reception
Road outside centre	Students not to leave site unaccompanied
Slippery grass and banks	Students briefed on arrival
Tennis courts	Students briefed on sensible use on arrival
Trip hazards on kerbs/steps	Students briefed on sensible behaviour on arrival
	Trip hazards painted to make them more obvious
Ski slope	Fenced off as out of bounds with warning signs
	Students briefed on arrival
Slippery surfaces when icy	Students briefed on arrival
	Grit used when necessary
Trailer area	Students briefed to be careful around trailers and not to touch them
	Trailers to be appropriately parked and secured
ADDITIONAL NOTES	
● Additional activities taking place in the centre grounds under visiting staff supervision, for example centre orienteering, should be based on this risk assessment with addition verbal details provided by the duty member of staff.	

Figure 6.2 Part of the SSRA for a residential facility at an adventure centre, North Yorkshire.

Daily risk assessment

In addition to the generic and site-specific risk assessments, both of which are usually done well in advance of a particular session, there should also be a daily or sessional risk assessment which considers the risks to a particular group at that location on a particular day. This would normally be done shortly before the activity is to start in order to have the most up-to-date information, particularly on the crucial variables of weather and personnel.

Typical issues to be factored into the daily risk assessment might include:

- weather forecast;
- underfoot conditions (such as ice);
- sea state or state of tide;
- daylight hours;
- river levels;
- injuries or illnesses;
- behavioural issues;
- staff expertise or staffing ratio;
- availability of communication or transport.

Many organisations deal with this level of risk assessment by means of a daily staff meeting, which, in addition to routine matters of logistics and communication, allows important decisions on risk management to be run past colleagues and managers. Such a meeting would often start with the current weather forecast being read out and then each leader in turn will be expected briefly to outline their plans for the day with an emphasis on any risk management issues. A typical outdoor centre meeting might go like this:

After hearing the forecast Sue, an experienced instructor, comments: 'My group are pretty strong and well motivated. The increasing wind is expected by mid-afternoon so I am happy for us to go along Crib Goch, but if it seems too strong at the start we can use the Miners' Track instead.'

Mike, a relatively junior instructor, is planning a kayak journey: 'Two of my group have painful blisters on their hands so we will just paddle the river from White Bridge to the lay by.'

A colleague adds: 'I did that section on Monday. Someone has thrown some old barbed wire into the east side of Fish Pool – you can avoid it by staying close to the other bank.'

This leads to a manager commenting: 'Just a reminder to everyone that we need to deal with blisters early, at the first hot spots – really, things have gone too far when the skin breaks.'

A third group, with John in charge, are planning a three-day mountain expedition, with high-level overnight camps. The longer duration and greater remoteness of this journey renders it more vulnerable to adverse weather or other constraints.

'One of the boys has been out of action with a throat infection for two days. The doc says he is OK to come with us, so I plan to camp at High Lake the first evening with a simple walk in from the road end in case we have any problems with him. Good phone signal at that camp too.'

'Day after, over Petticoat Hill and camp under the crag below the col, then on Day 3 over the col and back to the van.'

'John, I'm concerned that your Day 3 route is into the teeth of the forecast south-easterly gale and that col can be a pretty wild place when it's windy – can you come and discuss it with me after the meeting please?'

To my mind, this represents a mature and effective process of risk management. Of course, adventure centres have significant advantages in this respect. They usually have years of cumulative operation, at least a core of staff with detailed local knowledge and access to various resources such as vehicles and additional personnel to deal with unanticipated situations.

When leaders are operating in more informal situations without the structure and resources of such a centre, the daily meeting can still make great contributions to good practice by providing a forum for risk assessment and access to collective expertise. Ideally, leaders will have visited the activity sites to be used and, preferably, will have been involved in the preparation of the risk assessments to be used. When detailed local knowledge is lacking, some compensation can be made by careful research and preparation, but a generally cautious approach is desirable.

Skilled and experienced leaders can use sites unfamiliar to them and operate with risk assessments prepared by someone else but this is not ideal and not usually acceptable for leaders who do not have both the relevant leadership and technical skills to a high degree.

Finally, a leader operating alone, without any of the support and resources of colleagues and organisational structure, is especially vulnerable to unexpected difficulties or *force majeure*. Even when one has no immediate colleagues, an internal dialogue concerning the day's risk assessment has much to commend it. Demonstrably high levels of skill and experience, and the judgement associated with these, are necessary for the person who is in sole charge in this way.

Dynamic risk assessment

Once the activity has commenced there should be a constant monitoring and balancing of risks by the leader in the field – dynamic or continuous risk assessment. This latter represents one of the main duties of the party leader and can be best achieved by a flexible, observant and questioning approach:

- What could go wrong at the moment?

- What would happen if ... ?

- Are conditions deteriorating?

- Is the terrain as anticipated?

- How are the group coping with this activity?

- Who is having the most difficulty?

- Do I need to make any changes?

- Are we likely to run into any time problems?

Dynamic risk assessment. Would you trust this construction on the Trift Glacier?

A simple model such as the three circles of Task, Group and Individual (described by John Adair in *Action-Centred Leadership*) can help the leader to keep a properly broad view. Too many disasters have arisen from a blinkered approach which has a strong focus only on task – completing the voyage or winning the race – and which loses sight of individuals, the group and the effect that the environment has on them. The operating environment, be it sea or mountain, desert or forest, is of such importance that it is worth modifying the classic three circle model as in Figure 6.3 so that its context is given more prominence.

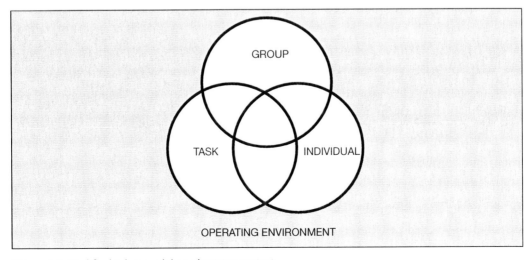

Figure 6.3 Modified Adair model emphasising context.

In summary, good practice in the provision of adventure activities would normally be expected to include the risk assessments outlined in Table 6.1. An organisation may use different terminology or different stages but the overall process should reflect this progressively sharper focus.

Table 6.1 The hierarchy of risk assessment

Risk assessment type	Scope	Written?	When done
Generic	A particular activity at any location	Yes	Well in advance
Site-specific	A particular activity at a particular location	Yes	Well in advance
Daily or sessional	The site-specific assessment customised for the conditions and group makeup on a particular day or for a particular session	Not usually	Immediately before a session starts
Dynamic	Ongoing risk assessment during the session	No	Ongoing during the session

How to produce a risk assessment

This advice mainly applies to the more formal generic and site-specific risk assessments which will usually result in a written document. A risk assessment tends to be as good as the person who prepares it. A person of broad and extensive experience of the activity being risk assessed will have seen similar activities delivered in a variety of ways and at a variety of locations. They will know what are the operational norms, will be tuned into the likely pattern of hazards and be familiar with what does and does not succeed as a control measure. It is to be hoped that they will also have the imagination and flexibility to identify less obvious hazards. For organisations subject to AALA licensing, the person of choice is the Technical Adviser for the activity – usually an individual with high-level national governing body qualifications in the chosen activity. For other aspects such as facilities or vehicles, an experienced manager might be the best choice.

Particularly for new activities, a team approach, with two or three individuals pooling their findings, can be highly effective. Also, if a person of the standing of a Technical Adviser is not available, then a combination of a person with high-level expertise in a different activity working in tandem with another who has good technical command of the activity in question can work well. Sometimes, the person who prepares a risk assessment is the person who designed, developed and delivered the activity and it can then be difficult for them to take an objective view.

Although some useful work can done with a paper and pencil exercise, a visit to the activity site or facility is almost essential for the preparation of a worthwhile risk assessment. The best information will come from seeing it in actual use, ideally by a real client group. For newly developed activities it is advisable to have made a preliminary assessment before a pilot operation with clients.

The assessor(s) should move around the site to gain different perspectives and, if time and other arrangements permit, can usefully seek the opinion of staff involved in the pilot. Notes are helpful and some people make a photographic record of elements that might be used for training purposes.

It is normal to indicate a date for future revision and update but any significant change in circumstances should trigger a revision and reissue. If a dam is constructed upstream, your carefully worked out risk assessment for gorge walking may have become obsolete or even dangerous if sudden releases of water from the dam have become a possible hazard. We should keep in mind the idea that risk assessment is a process and not a product, and that process should roll forwards.

Avoiding blind spots

It is necessary to decide what is an appropriate level of detail. I regard the development of a safe, effective field operation as the primary purpose of risk assessment. This is best achieved if our attention is focused on the most significant hazards and not distracted by dozens of trivial possibilities. It is easy for organisations to mistakenly identify the main priority of the risk assessment as generating documentary defences against litigation. Within such a culture the tendency is to list so many potential hazards of a minor nature that uncontrolled major risks can be obscured from view.

The greatest fear is the omission from our risk assessment, and consequently from our risk management, of a significant threat to life. Awareness of this should be a sobering influence on those responsible for risk management. In the accounts of outdoor tragedies it is not at all uncommon for key players to have ignored the specific hazard that ultimately resulted in a loss of life.

Just as an intense light can obscure our vision of something glowing less brightly, it is easy to lose sight of some of the day-to-day hazards that might be encountered. Outdoor instructors may have a highly tuned awareness of the hazards of sea, rock and river but are not always so alert to the more routine problems of the workplace. Falling downstairs may be less spectacular than falling down the Matterhorn, but the end result can be depressingly similar.

We operate in the wonderfully complex world of nature and some hazards are highly unpredictable or even unknowable. The devastating effect of the tragic tsunami of December 2004 had barely been anticipated, perhaps could not have been planned for, until the disaster itself updated our understanding. However, most serious omissions in adventure activities tend to concern hazards and situations that are well known and readily managed – we are dealing with failures of awareness and imagination, of training and communication. Risk assessment is the first step in bringing uncontrolled hazards into clear view.

How to use the result

First lock your filing cabinet and throw away the keys. Risk assessments are likely to be a complete waste of time and effort if they do not affect the way we operate; filing the written product away is one certain way to guarantee that they will never be read and so will not affect anything.

It is hard to pretend that risk assessments make exciting reading, but we should take every opportunity to get them read and to get them implemented. Most risk assessments fit extremely well into the processes by which we train and authorise staff because they usefully summarise some of the key hazards to be managed. They are a ready-made syllabus for relevant staff training, an agenda for productive staff discussions, a guide to the key areas of operation when senior staff make field observations of instructors, and an induction crash course for assistants and accompanying staff.

To emphasise the fact that risk assessment is process and not just product, the person who probably learns most is the one who does the risk assessment in the first place. When a revision is due, think about who can both contribute to and benefit from the process.

Closely linked to risk assessments is the use of scenario-based training, where a simulation of an emergency situation, or one

In Bardsey Sound – no place for man overboard . . .

needing prompt staff intervention, is used both to train staff and to validate or modify existing risk assessments. The closer the simulation is to field reality, the more relevant it will be. For example, man overboard training in sailing may often be done using a spare life jacket as the simulated casualty. This can be very illuminating with respect to boat handling and search skills but does not reveal the great difficulties that can exist in getting a real casualty who is floating alongside from the water and into the boat. A dummy of a realistic size and weight will be much closer to the real thing, and best of all might be to get a real person back into the boat, with the important proviso that this is done in closely controlled circumstances.

Outward Bound® periodically identifies an area of concern in its activity provision or an activity where risk management is particularly complex and then brings together a team of specialists to run a simulation, look at the issues and make recommendations. Although costly of staff time this is a powerful way of addressing apparently intractable problems and ensuring high standards in problematic areas of operation.

Chapter summary

- Risk assessment involves:

    - identifying hazards;
    - deciding who might be harmed;
    - evaluating the risks and existing precautions;
    - recording and periodically reviewing your findings .

- The main types in adventure activities are:

    - generic – a particular activity at any location;
    - site-specific – a particular activity a particular location;
    - daily or sessional – a particular activity with a particular group on a particular day;
    - continuous or dynamic – the leader's ongoing assessment of risk.

Chapter 7

Obligations of managers and providers

The boss

Being the leader in charge of a group when the weather is deteriorating and plans are beginning to unravel is a testing and worrying experience but, in my experience as the head of an outdoor centre, lying in bed at home and hearing the wind start to howl through the trees with a dozen or more groups out on expedition is uniquely stressful. The buck stops with you and although you will have undoubtedly put a great deal of thought and effort into staffing, into systems and into the abilities of your student population, at that moment your direct control is very limited. It sometimes feels like being the pillion passenger on a fast motor cycle and, in just the same way, you have no real alternative but to put your trust in the person who has direct hands-on control of the situation.

Finger on the pulse

Perhaps I have an over-developed imagination, but I have always felt that this level of empathy with what is going on in the field was an essential part of the job. The manager of an outdoor centre or the senior teacher responsible for an excursion must be close enough to the action to be aware, to some degree of specificity, what is happening or is planned to happen in the field, yet at the same time must have sufficient organisational distance to be able to take an overview and absorb the broad sweep of events.

Allocation of safety responsibility

Although the buck stops with you, some division of responsibility for safety is useful. As discussed in Chapter 5 it is desirable to have the practical management of risks delegated to a level close to the action. Staff need to know that they have your support and confidence and also what the limits of their responsibility are. For instance, we may quite reasonably give general authorisation for an instructor to be able to modify agreed plans in the face of adverse developments but are unlikely to give such blanket approval to a drastic increase in the level of challenge or risk over that originally planned.

Some organisations like to allocate specific safety responsibility to individuals. It is common in the field of outdoor management development for a group undergoing training to have a 'trainer' who oversees the process of their learning and a 'technician' who is responsible for the operation and safety of the activities in use. This can be very effective but it is important to ensure that the division of responsibility is clear and that important issues do not fall through the gap between each worker's area of control.

Having a person with specific safety responsibility, usually called a safety manager or similar, can also be effective, especially for larger organisations, but care should be taken to avoid diluting the unlimited personal responsibility for safety of each individual. An organisation is in trouble if it is believed that the safety manager is taking care of every aspect of safety and that nobody else need worry . . .

Related to this is the issue of span of control. Outdoor activities tend to be fairly complicated and often plans do change significantly. Anyone with supervisory responsibility for a number of groups in the field must be confident that they have sufficient information and sufficient control to be able to have a realistic influence on events.

Alarm bells

When the boss's sixth sense starts to signal all is not well, it is usually the time for action, perhaps a phone call to someone in the field or travelling to a vantage point to catch a glimpse of the action. I have great belief in the capabilities of instructors in the field and I am certainly not advocating that the manager is constantly on the phone to field staff, but the occasional contact when adverse influences are beginning to build is both prudent and likely to be well received by staff.

Walking the job

Managers always have too many demands on their time, but every effort should be made to get out in the field and see things happening. I have never dragged myself away from the desk to do this and then felt afterwards that my time would actually have been better spent in the office.

Impromptu visits always give you an interesting perspective on what is happening and the rapport with field staff tends to be outstandingly good. If you are sharing a canoe or a belay ledge with a leader, they will have a directness and informality of access to the boss that is very hard to establish in an office, and you will then hear what their safety concerns really are. Staff soon catch on to bosses who are only seen in perfect conditions – try to drop in on one of those really horrible days, if only to see the reaction.

Early in my first job as an instructor, I was camping with a group on Esk Hause, a pass high in the English Lake District. It was a wet and windy night and next morning the cloud was down below sea level. As I peered out of the door of my own tent I could just make out another very small tent, about 50 metres from our position, that had not been there the previous evening. This was unexpected and one of my students, who was already up and about, went to investigate. 'Oh, it's just the Warden cooking sausages,' he announced. I suppose the boss was checking up on me, but it never felt like that, and I and the group were thrilled that he, no longer a young man, had made the long trek in the small hours, evidently just to say 'Hello' and cook a few sausages on his Primus stove!

Unfortunately, when you get back from your stimulating visit to the coal face your duties and obligations are still waiting for you . . .

Obligations of providers

The provider or leader of adventurous activities has a clear legal and moral duty of care towards his or her charges. When we are working with minors we are often *in loco parentis* and expected to give similar care to that expected from a prudent parent.

Legal

Every country will have its own laws applying to the provision of outdoor activities. Some of these will be of general applicability to any enterprise, others will be specific to adventure sports.

The Health and Safety at Work Act 1974

The UK Health and Safety at Work Act places general duties of care on employers and the self-employed to conduct their undertakings without risk to the health and safety of others. This legislation applies directly to most commercial enterprises. Although some individuals or groups (unpaid volunteers for instance) might technically be exempt from this legislation, HSE considers it good practice for those who carry out such activities to provide the same level of health and safety protection as they would if they were duty holders under the Act.

In the event of serious injury or death the provider will inevitably be compared with the body of accepted good practice and much of this will have been at least influenced if not governed by health and safety legislation. Although the legal duty lies with the employer this does not exempt employees from their own responsibilities to operate in conformance with the employer's advice.

The Act also places certain duties on any person to provide plant and equipment which is safe, so far as is reasonably practicable, for use by other people.

The Management of Health and Safety at Work Regulations 1999

Alongside the Act, the Management of Health and Safety at Work Regulations 1999 (HSWA) make a specific requirement that suitable and sufficient risk assessments are carried out to assess the risks to employees or others that may be harmed, and to determine the control measures necessary to reduce these risks to a tolerable level. More on the use of this important tool can be found in Chapter 6. When an establishment has more than five employees there is a requirement for a written safety policy and for a written description of the safety arrangements to be used.

The Regulations also require effective management and the Health and Safety Executive (HSE) promote a model with the following core elements:

- Developing policy
- Organising
- Planning and implementation
- Measuring performance
- Reviewing performance
- Auditing.

These usefully summarise the general functions of managers.

The Adventure Activities Licensing Regulations 1996

Following the 1993 tragedy at Lyme Bay on the English South Coast where four young people lost their lives while under instruction in an introductory kayak session, Parliament enabled legislation. The Activity Centres (Young Persons' Safety) Act 1995 and the Adventure Activities Licensing Regulations 1996 require the inspection and licensing of providers of adventure activities to those under 18 years of age.

The activities to be regulated were to be those that included some or all of the following factors that contributed to the occurrences at Lyme Bay, namely:

- the whole group may be endangered if things go wrong and there may be a significant risk of death;
- the competence of instructors is a crucial part of safe operation;
- the activity is vulnerable to changes in the weather or the natural environment;
- above all, failures of safety management were seen as being of the highest importance and the focus of the legislation reflects this.

After the passage of the Regulations a licensing authority – the Adventure Activities Licensing Authority (AALA) – was established. The best description of their duties and operation is to be found in the Guidance to the Licensing Authority from the Health and Safety Commission and published by HSE Books.

AALA is funded by the Department for Education and Skills and providers are also charged for inspections and for the processing of an initial and detailed written application. There is a core inspectorate of about eight senior inspectors and a typical inspection might involve two of them visiting the provider's base and operating sites over 3–6 hours. Particular attention is paid to interviewing staff, to management systems and, wherever possible, to the direct observation of the actual adventure activities.

After inspection AALA has the following main options:

- issue of a licence;
- issue of a licence but with the provider being required or advised to accomplish certain changes in their methods or systems;
- withholding the licence until such works have been completed;
- refusal of a licence.

It is rare for a licence to be refused. Licences are issued for a period to be decided by AALA, usually from one to three years, and dependent on the scale of operation of the provider. The main activities covered are listed in Table 7.1.

Table 7.1 Main activities covered by AALA licensing

Climbing	Watersports	Trekking	Caving
Rock climbing	Canoeing	Hillwalking	Caving
Abseiling	Kayaking	Mountaineering	Pot-holing
Ice climbing	Dragon boating	Fell running	Mine exploration
Gorge walking	Wave skiing	Orienteering	
Ghyll scrambling	White-water rafting	Pony trekking	
Sea level traversing	Improvised rafting	Off-road cycling	
	Sailing	Off-piste skiing	
	Sailboarding		
	Windsurfing		

When a provider applies for an AALA license and offers some activities that are out of scope of the regulations – a ropes course would be an example – then the AALA inspection will usually take an interest in the entire provision and not just those activities that are in scope. Their comments and opinions on out-of-scope activities do not carry regulatory force but any signals of unsatisfactory arrangements (such as poor construction or operation of a ropes course) would attract adverse comment from AALA and they are permitted to refer any serious concerns to the Health and Safety Executive who may then intervene.

Exemptions

Activities on this list may not require a licence if they are of a limited scope. An example of this might be the provision of kayaking on a small inland body of water less than 100 metres in width. The Regulations only apply to those offering activities to those of 18 years and under so providers who limit their provision to adults are exempt from the control of this legislation (though probably not from the Health and Safety at Work Act). Curiously, some of the most important exemptions:

- voluntary associations

- educational establishments

- the armed services

- Northern Ireland, the Isle of Man and the Channel Islands

- children accompanied by their parent

include some of the groups that have featured prominently in major accidents during the provision of adventure activities. Often, these groups will subscribe to non-statutory schemes of accreditation operated by particular groupings of providers.

An adult trekking group – exempt from AALA licensing.

It is not clear that this exemption has been a benefit to voluntary associations and educational establishments. As mentioned above, in the event of things going badly wrong the provider is measured against established good practice and, to avoid damaging legal action or a serious loss of reputation, must not be found wanting. In my opinion, organisations that are exempt from the letter of the Regulations would be unwise not to make efforts closely to match the standards that apply to license holders.

Has it worked?

The initial appointment of the Licensing Authority raised eyebrows since it was under the management of a private company which had previously operated a hotel grading scheme. However, the company was careful to appoint highly experienced outdoor specialists as the Authority's inspectors. This did much to reassure the outdoor industry who were already smarting a little at being subjected to a draconian scheme of special licensing that had previously been reserved for evidently hazardous activities such as the work of mines and quarries or the nuclear industry. The Health and Safety Executive (well aware of their existing powers under HSWA) were noticeably lukewarm about the need for additional legislation specific to the outdoor industry.

Although there was much talk of sledgehammers and nuts, outdoor providers have learned to live with the Licensing Regulations and many have found that, by developing an effective rapport with inspectors, much wise comment and good advice may be had. There is little doubt that, both by direct and indirect influence, AALA has had a positive effect on safety standards in the provision of adventure activities but it is much less clear whether these benefits are proportionate to the considerable cost and effort involved. Reputable providers (of which there are many) continue to put a great deal of effort into a focused approach to risk management, and there is little doubt that they would do so without the requirements of licensing, but a small minority of others muddle along as they always have. Tragedies still occur, some due to terrible misfortune but others springing from the most basic ignorance of good practice.

In launching a consultation in 2003 the government has made it clear that they expect the Licensing Scheme to continue but are also open to suggestions for its evolution into a non-statutory scheme, for alternative methods of funding and for its extension to some currently exempt groups.

In 2006 a research project was commissioned by the Adventure Activities Industry Advisory Committee (AAIAC) to:

- examine the various non-statutory accreditation schemes that apply to adventure activities;

- identify sectors within the field that operate without any such accreditation;

- identify whether it might be possible to integrate individual schemes under the umbrella of a benchmark standard applicable across the field.

Other legislation

Other legislation that has a bearing upon the safety of participants and staff includes that governing fire regulations, vehicles, food hygiene, the protection of children and the structural security and safety of facilities and equipment. Although not confined to the provision of outdoor activities, deficiencies in these areas can have a devastating effect which, in the worst cases, can generate multiple fatalities.

Vehicles

The use of vehicles such as minibuses may require the driver to hold a specific form of driving licence and may be subject to additional requirements on speed limits and loading. When pool vehicles are used there will need to be careful control of vehicle checks and maintenance.

The law requires the wearing of seat belts in most circumstances and this should be actively implemented and policed by staff. It is desirable for loose equipment and rucksacks to be isolated in an internal cage or carried in a trailer or on a roof rack.

The largest single influence on vehicle safety is undoubtedly the driver. Many staff in outdoor operations are younger drivers. This is an age group that is not well regarded by insurers, and managers should put great effort into keeping the issue of driving safety at the forefront of day-to-day operation.

Equipment

Every instructor and every manager will know that good equipment and clothing is important to the safety of adventure activities. It is normal to distinguish between general clothing and equipment and that which is safety critical. Critical safety equipment might include helmets, karabiners, climbing harnesses, ropes and life jackets.

However, even a prosaic piece of clothing or equipment can have great importance, especially in severe conditions. If you are lost in bad weather a faulty compass is a life-threatening liability; if the zip on your waterproof jacket fails in the middle of a storm, it is more than a minor inconvenience. Planning must assume that the worst possible conditions are, sooner or later, going to happen.

Critical safety equipment must be regularly checked against defined criteria and will also have an identified working life which may be expressed in days of actual use or total lifetime. It is prudent to apply checks to non-critical equipment too.

Employers are expected to conform to the requirements of the Personal and Protective Equipment at Work Regulations 1992. Personal and protective equipment (PPE) covers equipment and clothing which is intended to protect employees against the hazards they might meet in the workplace. Employers are required to provide PPE and may not charge for its use.

Importantly, PPE should not normally be seen as the primary defence against hazards. For instance, if there is a hazard of loose rock at a rock climbing site, you are expected to reduce the hazard to a tolerable level by removing the loose rock or controlling access to certain areas. It is definitely not acceptable to say to your instructor, 'The rock fall is really bad – here is your helmet.'

The PPE regulations expect the employer to:

- select and issue suitable PPE;
- instruct staff in its use;
- ensure proper use;
- store and maintain the equipment properly.

In Europe, such equipment will usually have a CE marking (Conformité Européene) which is an indication by the manufacturer that it is fit for its specified purpose.

Reporting of accidents

In addition to the value in identifying and learning from accidents as described in Chapter 13, there is a UK legal requirement to report certain categories of work-related accident under RIDDOR – the Reporting of Injuries Diseases and Dangerous Occurrence Regulations 1995. The regulations specify the need to report:

- death or major injury;
- injury resulting in more than three days of absence from work;
- reportable diseases (an example in the outdoor field would be leptospirosis – which can, on rare occasions, be contracted during water activities);
- dangerous occurrences (including serious near misses).

The requirements apply to both employees and clients of outdoor providers.

Child protection

Following the Children Act 1989 and the Education Act 2002, the UK Department for Education and Skills (DfES) expects the governing bodies of schools to make the necessary arrangements for:

- child protection;
- safe recruitment;
- dealing with allegations.

They are expected to identify a senior person who is the child protection contact. When schools use third-party providers to supply adventure activities, similar safeguards will be sought. More information is to be found in Chapter 3.

Insurance

Employers are legally required to hold employers' liability insurance as protection against claims from employees. Public liability insurance will give protection against claims from third parties as a result of injury (or death) or harm done to property as a result of any of your business activities. A typical sum in 2006 is about £5 million cover. Although public liability insurance may not be a legal requirement, many potential customers, particularly organisations such as schools or companies, will require it to be held by a supplier of services, and most providers will want to hold it.

Civil liability insurance gives a wider level of cover than normal third-party and usually provides indemnity against errors and omissions in instruction or advice and would include person to person claims. Some operators, such as mountain guides, are required by their professional body to hold this cover, and many coaches and instructors consider it to be necessary.

Insurers can sometimes treat adventure activities as an unreasonably risky business and apply restrictive clauses to the cover they provide. It is desirable to get to know your insurer and for them to become familiar with the way your business operates and how risks are managed. A few specialist brokers will have established expertise within the field and can be expected to give good advice on the level and nature of insurance cover required, as can professional bodies.

Records

Keeping adequate records can be of considerable value if it proves necessary to revisit the arrangements. The main focus for this is often in connection with potential litigation. The general rule is that any claim for personal injury must be commenced in court within three years of the date of the injury with the proviso that when a child is injured the three-year time limit does not begin to run until the child's eighteenth birthday is reached.

In any claim of this kind it is important to have any original records of the incident, including statements by those involved, photographs, inspection reports, any retained equipment and so on.

Chapter summary

- Managers should understand field operations and be ready to intervene.
- Walking the job is especially important.
- Legal requirements are wide and varied but centrally include:
    - the Health and Safety at Work Act;
    - adventure activity licensing through AALA.
- Licensing excludes certain activities and categories of provider.
- Other relevant legislation covers vehicles, personal protective equipment and the reporting of accidents and unsafe occurrences.
- Liability insurance exists for:
    - public liability;
    - civil liability;
    - employer's liability.

Chapter 8

Advice to teachers, leaders and instructors

Pattern recognition

So how does it all go wrong? We have all heard the phrase 'an accident waiting to happen' and it is certainly the case that, when things go badly wrong, like a baleful Greek tragedy played out against the backdrop of sea or mountains, there is a sense of inevitability in the way adverse influences accumulate. But for all this appearance of inevitability, of logical stepwise escalation, it is elusively difficult to spot what is happening when you are an actor in the proceedings, not a disinterested observer.

Recognition of pattern in the development of a situation in the outdoors is one of the most effective ways of developing an awareness of the wider situation. One of the reasons that 'experience', especially for the leader, is such an important influence on the success of an adventure is that experienced individuals have an extensive collection of previous situations (and, importantly, also their outcomes) with which to compare present reality. On a computer this would be called an 'expert system' but, with enough effort and commitment, we can all develop, between our ears, a superbly portable version of the same thing. A familiarity with these patterns is an important part of what we call judgement. Some of the more commonly occurring patterns are described in this chapter and every active outdoor leader will have found themselves in at least a few of these scenarios.

Experience and pattern recognition

Aire de Geuss, a future gazer and strategist for Shell, described at an Outward Bound® conference an example of the need for a foundation of previous experience to support pattern recognition.

> Around the year 1900, a highly intelligent tribal leader was taken from his 'undiscovered' stone age life in the jungle to see a bustling oriental city. He had never left his home village before and now saw trains, steamships, the telegraph, towering buildings and many other

manifestations of developed urban life, yet these evidently left him unmoved. The one thing that impressed him was a simple handcart – 'a man carrying more bananas than I have ever seen carried before'. (de Geuss, 1991)

His previous experience had not given any point of reference against which he could measure the significance of most of the achievements of the city – but he did understand about carrying bananas and could therefore appreciate the technology of a simple wheeled vehicle. The 'obvious' is only apparent to those with appropriate prior experience (an argument, incidentally, for experiential education, since it allows those taking part to accumulate new experiences in what is often a playful situation).

Failing to see the whole picture

We see a more tragic demonstration of the need for pattern recognition when inexperienced leaders fail to pick up the signals of a nascent situation of danger that would have been all too obvious to an experienced peer. 'But everyone was laughing and having a fantastic time, it just came out of the blue,' they protest against the injustice of a cruel fate but, in reality, long before disaster struck, the alarm bells were already ringing – but only for ears trained to hear them.

And so one of the generic patterns that leads to catastrophe is that of failing to see the whole picture, and particularly a failure to realise that escalation is upon you. It is strikingly common for tragedies to grow stepwise from innocuous beginnings; chaos theory tells us that in complex systems tiny influences can have profound consequences.

For want of a nail, the shoe was lost; For want of the shoe, the horse was lost; For want of the horse, the rider was lost; For want of the rider, the battle was lost; For want of the battle, the kingdom was lost; And all for the want of a nail. (Benjamin Franklin)

Trying to please other people

Most of us like to be popular. Trying to please other people is often a desirable thing to do, but an analysis of serious outdoor incidents reveals that it is commonly a factor in blurring priorities or distorting judgement. Instructors, anxious to give a memorable day, are especially vulnerable to this influence; resolving a difficult decision by bowing to the wishes of one's charges can be irresistibly attractive to incautious or unimaginative leaders. Sometimes it is necessary to disappoint in order to bow to more pressing priorities.

Perceived time pressure

Another favourite distraction from the proper priorities is that of rushing against the clock. Usually, these pressures are self-imposed by the leader and are easily avoided once you have realised that they have come to bear on a situation. A headlong rush at the end of a day can be exhilarating but it is also a time when our guard drops and when fatigue can make people more vulnerable.

I had a close escape from such a mismanagement of priorities in Scotland many years ago when leading two winter climbers on a cliff called Stob Coire nan Lochan high above Glencoe. We were staying at a residential centre which was very comfortable but where the chef was a particularly plain speaking character who took pride in closing the dining room at 6:30 pm sharp and who would give a tongue lashing to anyone who was late. Back on the mountain, we had enjoyed an excellent climb and were sitting on the summit enjoying Glencoe's unique panorama when I glanced at my watch and realised in horror that we were in danger of being late for supper and of facing the wrath of the chef.

After about 15 minutes of running pell-mell down the mountain, on far from simple ground, a sensible thought finally entered my head. Missing dinner or displeasing the chef were both unattractive outcomes but it had now dawned on me that I was risking something much worse. We slowed down and some time later faced down our tormentor – and got dinner too.

It is worth noting that the revelation that the risk escalator was beginning to roll resulted from stepping outside the immediate picture to take a wider and more objective view. To do so will usually give the leader a helpful, often an essential, perspective on the situation.

Being blinded by the prize

Some activities or objectives gain a particular status as a thing to do. Many practitioners in adventure activities enjoy the 'having done' more than the 'doing'; once certain passages gain a bar room kudos they become irresistible. When one is a short way from completion it can be desperately hard to turn back. It is hard to imagine most of the Everest climbers in the 1996 disaster so well described in the pages of *Into Thin Air* acting in the same way, pressing on regardless, on some unknown hill in Norway. The distorting effect of the 'big tick' was well known to the ancients:

> When the archer shoots for no particular prize, he has all his skills. When he shoots to win a brass buckle, he is already nervous; when he shoots for a gold prize, he goes blind, sees two targets, and is out of his mind. His skill has not changed, but the prize divides him. He cares! He thinks more of winning than of shooting, and the need to win drains him of power. (Chuang Tzu)

And, one might add, of judgement too.

In the sphere of adventure education the enthusiasm of youngsters can be triggered by talking up the activities, often by the use of dramatic names. Every child in the school wants to have done the Big Swing, the Death Slide or the Washing Machine. This supports energetic participation but it also puts pressure on the leader to deliver – nobody wants to go back to school to say, 'Well, we didn't do it – it was a bit cold' or 'The rock was too slippery'. All proven outdoor leaders will have encountered this pressure. Most learn that there are often circumstances where the ambitions of participants must be tempered and where alternative activities must be undertaken, but sometimes this additional pressure can tip the balance.

False assumptions will get you in the end

'Well, is it safe?' is the question everybody asks, as though all activities fell neatly either side of some indisputable line between the horrifically dangerous and the entirely benign. Of course what we are almost always engaging with is a calculated risk. Calculated risk – an interesting phrase. Its first part implies precision, exactitude, yet the second reminds us that we are dealing with uncertainties. Even at best, with good information we may confidently assess and identify risks but there is no guarantee that the highly unlikely will not occur. Bookmakers' odds numerically represent the likelihood of particular outcomes but nobody would take an interest in betting on a horse race if the 40 to 1 outsider never won.

So we can make a confident and careful assessment of hazards and control measures, judge an activity to be 'low risk' and yet an unlikely turn of events can still result in an accident. When our calculations are based on false assumptions they are even less reliable.

The *Fiona McDonald*

Outward Bound® had a painful reminder of this with one of its cutters – wonderful, traditional, heavy, but un-decked sailing boats. These craft had been sailed for forty years without serious mishap and even deliberate efforts to turn a boat over at its moorings by swamping, pulling ropes fixed to the masthead, rocking from side to side and so on had failed to produce a capsize.

On a blustery spring day on a Scottish sea loch a group of staff were developing their boat handling skills. An inexperienced helmsman was on the tiller under close supervision. Let us look at an extract from a report written a few days later:

> John was just considering giving the order to go about when the boat was struck by an unusually strong gust or squall which had been seen coming along the loch. At about the same time, the bosun felt a strong gust shake the boathouse and went outside to check on the boats. The consensus of estimates is that this wind reached Force 7 or 8.

> *Fiona McDonald* was already heeled in the windy conditions so, when the gust struck, the angle of heel increased considerably and the boat began to ship water over the gunwale. John encouraged Ben to push the tiller away in order to bring the boat into the wind and shouted to spill wind from the mainsail. The responses probably did not take effect until the gunwale was in the water and had no apparent effect on the increasing heel of the boat. John describes the movement of the boat as 'gentle but continuous' but it was soon clear to him that a capsize was inevitable. He shouted to the crew to 'Get out!' and helped Ben who was clinging determinedly to the tiller. As the mast and sails struck the water the movement continued unimpeded until the boat was completely inverted. One of the crew scrambled directly over the windward gunwale on to the upper surface of the hull thus remaining dry. The rest, including John and Ben were in the water supported by the lifejackets or buoyancy

aids that all wore. All scrambled or were pulled on to the upper surface of the hull. John confirmed that all were accounted for and uninjured and also warned the crew of the dangers of trapping fingers in the centreplate casing. There had been no panic and evacuation had been well controlled. All emergency equipment was inaccessible beneath the capsized hull. (Barton, 1998)

In my view, it is very important for staff to be able to 'push the envelope' during training of this kind and to find out the limits of their own and their equipment's capabilities – but this was evidently happening to a greater degree than was realised at the time. Further on, the conclusions of the report include this comment:

There appears to have been a widely held and insidious underlying belief that the cutters 'did not capsize'. This is perhaps understandable for such solid vessels but we believe that future use of the vessels will now benefit from a recognition that, in adverse circumstances, capsizes can occur. Excessive reliance seems to have been placed on the results of 'swamp testing' in 1991 during which it proved impossible to capsize a cutter deliberately.

I hardly need to point out that the false assumption that the vessel was 'uncapsizable' led to the emergency equipment being located where it could not be reached in the event of the exact emergency for which it was provided! With the perfect vision of hindsight this was clearly ridiculous – and every sailor knows that any boat can capsize if pressed hard enough. We were lucky to get these lessons at so low a price. The emergency equipment was relocated! In addition, for future journeys, the effective sail area of the vessel was reduced by taking sails such as the flying jib out of the sail wardrobe and removing the bowsprit.

It is worth noting that this incident took place shortly after Outward Bound® had introduced comprehensive reporting of near miss incidents. Discussions after the capsize revealed that, on rare occasions extending over many years, other cutter skippers had been surprised by green water coming over the gunwales but this had not been reported at the time and had thus not become widely known. If a system to report near misses had been in place (see Chapter 13) at the time of these occurrences it is possible that the capsize might have been averted by an earlier realisation that, in certain conditions, the vessels were capable of capsize.

If something can go wrong, in time it probably will

Statistics are unforgiving. In a large operation, the frequency with which activity occurs greatly multiplies the likelihood of unlikely events actually occurring. Although we can rarely apply numerical odds to outdoor events, imagine that something undesirable, say a large tree branch falling into the activity area, has a 1000 : 1 chance of occurring during an activity session. We may at first sight regard these as relatively favourable odds; however, run the session twice weekly and in a year the odds of one of the sessions going wrong drops to about 10 : 1. (The odds of any individual session meeting misfortune, of course, remain at 1000 : 1.)

One of the primary purposes of risk assessment is not to simply focus on the obvious hazards but to identify and appraise more unlikely events before the mill of statistics can act on them and generate an unwanted incident.

A painful example of the unlikely event happening can be seen in the case of a rope swing – an exciting pendulum swing built into a ropes course. The participant, at this point sitting in the high fork of a tree, would clip her harness on to a loop at the end of the pendulum rope and then launch in a spine tingling swing into space. This activity had been built by an experienced instructor who paid great attention to the detail and security of the construction. Risk assessments were done, the activity was put into regular use and judged a great success. It was a great example of an activity which gave an exciting perception of risk but which was considered to be, in reality, very safe.

The loop at the end of the pendulum rope was tied with a figure of eight knot with, for additional security, a further stopper knot. This is a very safe and well proven method. However, one way in which knots can start to unravel is if the unused rope at the tail of the knot is left too short, so the careful builder of the swing left a generous 15 cm.

After some months of successful operation another instructor decided, during a routine check, to tidy up the tail of the knot by taping it down snugly – a matter of aesthetics rather than one of safety. Unfortunately, this taping was not done along the entire length of the tail but confined to its extremity. Over the next few weeks of use the taped section began to creep and a loop, a false loop held only by adhesive tape, developed between the tail and the main rope. This was, quite literally, an accident waiting to happen.

Eventually, perhaps inevitably, a participant in the tree fork erroneously clipped the false loop. The instructor checking the attachment from an adjoining branch failed to notice this because the participant's hand was obscuring the true loop and, with the error uncorrected, the participant launched into space. The tape ripped immediately and the person on the swing crashed to the ground sustaining serious injuries from which, fortunately, a full recovery was made.

It is worth noting that the serious outcome of this incident required several failings or oversights to occur in sequence:

● the rope arrangement being modified (by taping) without full consideration being given to the consequences of this action;

● the failure of routine risk assessments to identify and correct this potential hazard (a few pennyworth of tape to completely cover the tail would have effectively eliminated the hazard);

● an error of supervision by the instructor at the final security check.

Such a sequence might be considered to be very unlikely to occur and yet the situation developed as described. When we plan and design activities we must remember that occasional fallibility is the human condition.

The myth of instructor invulnerability

In my experience, instructors and leaders are strongly committed to ensuring their clients' safety. They may not always be able to meet this goal as well as everyone would wish but it is most unusual to find an individual who does not pay great attention to taking good care of those in their charge. This makes it even more surprising to find that it is not uncommon for instructors to be somewhat careless of their own safety.

Perhaps it is the wearing of an instructor T-shirt or badge that persuades some people that they have become invulnerable. In fact, it appears that instructors (and, particularly, young instructors) are more likely to be involved in serious injury than are course particpants. It is very important for staff safety to be prominent in the culture of an organisation, through training, induction and regular reminders to field staff by managers. It is also vitally important that leaders and instructors do not themselves fall into the trap of assuming invulnerability.

Two particular situations when instructors are at risk stand out. The first of these is the preparation or rigging of a site before an activity session begins (or its equivalent when the site is de-rigged). Here the instructor is often under time pressure (perceived or actual), is not under the eye of clients (and so, perhaps, may be more inclined to take short cuts) and may be working alone. These are all adverse influences. Lone working in potentially hazardous locations is to be avoided and will soon be subject to legislation in the workplace.

This instructor is secured with a prussik loop while rigging this climbing site, in order to protect himself against a possible slip.

The second is when instructors are the victim of assaults by aggrieved or frustrated participants. The value of adventure education in helping individuals who present challenging behaviour has often been demonstrated but, in the rare cases when violent attacks occur, the instructor or leader is entirely in the front line at the focal point of exploding frustration.

It is extremely important that staff who might find themselves in this situation are appropriately trained and supported. Inexperienced instructors can easily inflame a situation and a consistently calm approach which defuses rather than inflames conflict has much to recommend it.

Positive and negative influences

Experienced leaders develop a sixth sense of when the odds are beginning to stack up against them and they will automatically see an event in the wider context. Those not so experienced are much less likely to see the signals outlined above and tend to see minor setbacks in isolation rather than as bricks in a growing wall. It can be helpful to keep a kind of mental checklist to monitor where the balance of positive and negative influences lies at a particular point in an excursion.

Good judgement is encouraged by:

- wide experience of the activity;
- wide experience of leadership and instruction;
- a reflective, thoughtful approach;
- appropriate planning and preparation;
- good knowledge of the party and the capabilities of its members;
- the study of the experiences of others, especially when things go wrong;
- planning in the expectation that not everything will go according to plan;
- making mistakes and learning from them.

Good judgement is jeopardised by:

- fatigue, cold, exhaustion;
- hostile weather;
- over reliance on the possibility of help;
- lack of food;
- trying to please other people;
- perceived time pressure leading to inappropriate haste;
- over-ambition;
- poor planning and preparation;
- false assumptions;
- a failure to notice that 'apparent risk' is becoming 'real risk';
- alcohol;
- a 'macho' approach;
- determination to get home at all costs.
- over-confidence;

A healthy attitude to risk management recognises that every leader will occasionally make errors of judgement and uses these as the basis for further learning and development.

If you find that the list of negative influences is building up it is probably time to give some serious thought to a change of plan. On a lighter note, the Scottish Mountaineering Club used to publish a general guide to walking in the magnificent Scottish mountains which ended with a list similar to the above giving the main causes of mountain accidents, including over-ambition, excessive use of alcohol, a late start and failure to consult map and compass, and so on. A friend of mine maintains that in the 1960s the members of the university mountaineering club at St Andrew's owed some of their best days to a determined campaign to embrace the maximum number of these foolhardy actions in a single day!

Judgement tools – a matrix

Not every method works for every leader so it is worth trying a few different approaches. An extension of the idea (Williamson and Meyer 2003) of a checklist of positive and negative influences starts from the observation that serious incidents usually will involve a combination of some or all of the following:

- unsafe conditions;

- unsafe acts;

- unsafe perception.

A situation where a leader is facing two of the above at the same time is particularly threatening. All three wins some kind of malevolent jackpot.

Unsafe conditions might include unsafe, inappropriate or unsuitable:

- falling objects;
- adverse weather;
- equipment or clothing;
- swift or cold water;
- unsuitable physical or psychological makeup

- snow conditions;
- vehicles;
- medication;
- ratio or size of group;
- fatigue;
- support;

- lack of relevant training or experience;
- false assumptions;
- hostile animals;
- hygiene;
- operating system.

Unsafe acts might include unsafe, inadequate or inappropriate:

- position;
- protection;
- construction;

- instruction;
- supervision;
- procedure;

- speed;
- spacing;
- communication.

Unsafe perception leading to errors of judgement as a result of inappropriate or unsafe:

- desire to please others;
- misreading the situation;
- perceived time pressure;
- failure to recognise new situation;

- distraction;
- ignoring instincts;
- attitude;
- leadership style;

- complacency;
- over-ambition;
- priorities.

I tend to operate at a more intuitive level and find that I struggle a little with allocating something that I know to be unsafe to a particular category of conditions, acts or perceptions so I do not often use this as a practical field tool. Others do and it is certainly worth consideration.

How accidents happen

One of the mysteries in the way accidents happen is their often arbitrary appearance. Leaders can habitually operate to very high standards and yet still have an accident happen. Others may appear to lurch along from crisis to crisis yet never experience more than minor incidents. I am in no doubt that in the long run, 'safe' operators have fewer serious accidents than less careful ones, but this is scant consolation to the good leader for whom things have gone badly wrong.

One model of the occurrence of incidents that was developed by James Reason when he was he was Professor of Psychology at the University of Manchester is rather persuasive in explaining this phenomenon. It looks at the trajectory of opportunity that has to be established before an accident occurs (see Figure 8.1).

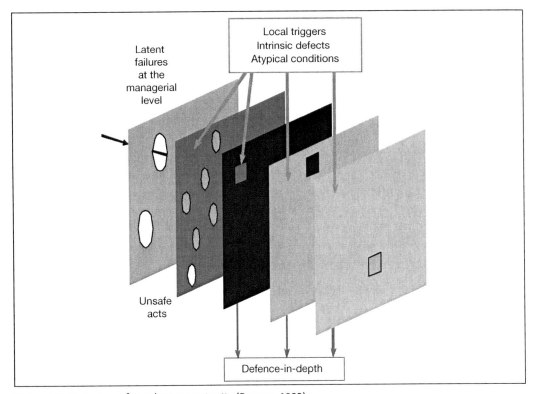

Figure 8.1 Trajectory of accident opportunity (Reason, 1993).

The first barrier represents the obstacle that our risk management arrangements have put in the way of the accident trajectory. None of our arrangements are likely to be 100 per cent reliable in every aspect so there are some holes in the barrier and it is useful to imagine these holes moving about on the barrier as conditions and circumstances change.

Next in line is a further barrier where our working practice guards against hazards. Occasional unsafe acts pierce this barrier with holes. Further barriers exist which are based on the intrinsically 'safe' locations that we use, weather conditions that we choose and so on, but each of these can in turn be pierced by holes open to the accident trajectory as atypical conditions occur. Grossly atypical conditions (such as a major storm) might make some of these holes rather large (see Figure 8.2).

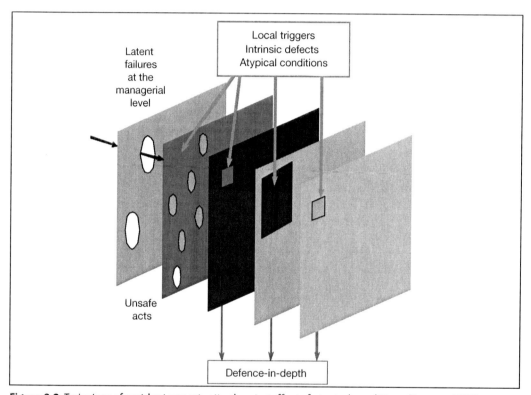

Figure 8.2 Trajectory of accident opportunity showing effect of atypical conditions (Reason, 1993).

It is easy to imagine labels that we might apply to some of these barriers in an outdoor context. In rock climbing, the belay system, the quality of the rock and a safe landing might all be barriers to an accident occurring; defects in any of these areas produce the holes for the trajectory of accident opportunity to become complete (see Figure 8.3).

This model corresponds closely to my own instinctual understanding of what is happening in the field when we start to manage complex adventure undertakings. I recommend it to you for consideration.

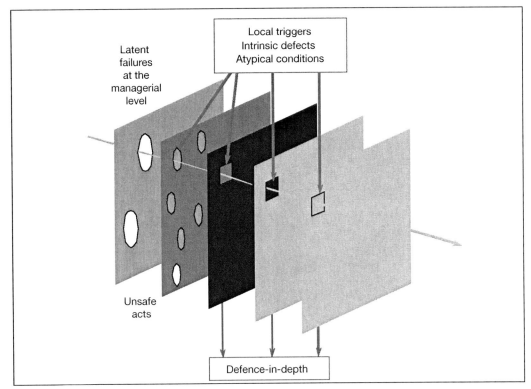

Figure 8.3 Completed trajectory of accident opportunity (Reason, 1993).

You are the problem!

When you look at the records of incidents in many adventure activities you are likely to get the impression that poor equipment, bad luck, unexpected bad weather and various freak occurrences are the prime cause of most accidents. Although rarely identified, human factors are in fact the major influence on the occurrence of serious incidents. It may be a peculiarly British trait to suppress the importance of such uncomfortable things but we tend to neglect human factors in training, selection and in our entire method of operation.

Despite the title of this section, this issue is not about incompetent leaders – far from it. The problem is that we are all human animals and although we may like to see ourselves as logical and consistent in our actions, the truth is that there is a streak of irrationality in all of us, and the influence of the more subterranean aspects of our personalities can at times be hugely powerful.

Commitment is a straitjacket

Take a very simple example that every leader will recognise. When we plan an activity or visit we often have a main plan and a fallback plan to be actuated in the event of adverse conditions or other problems. These are often called Plan A and Plan B and on the face of it everything appears perfectly simple. As soon as things start to be a little testing on Plan A the leader shifts to Plan B – simple and obvious! Unfortunately, the reality is a little different and it often proves to be surprisingly difficult to take this simple step. I thought that perhaps this was my problem only, but on consulting colleagues I found we all seem to find this difficult – with the result that leaders cling to Plan A for longer than logic or good practice might dictate.

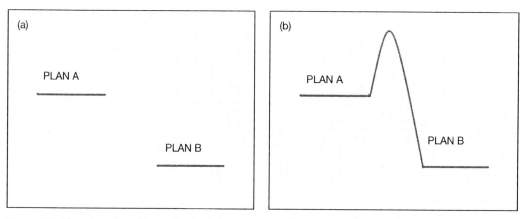

Figure 8.4 Changing plans. The vertical axis is a measure of how un-comfortable the leader feels.

Figure 8.4 represents how difficult this step is. Instead of comfortably slipping from Plan A to Plan B (Figure 8.4(a)) there is a large barrier of resistance to be surmounted (Figure 8.4(b)). Why on earth should this be? The answer seems to be that at a subconscious level most of us are so strongly attached to a view of ourselves as rational and consistent beings, that although logic dictates a rapid shift to Plan B, our instincts tell us otherwise. We feel the transfer is not the right thing to do since it shatters out image of pure consistency of action.

How certain can you be?

When I was a student I was lucky enough to join a group on an expedition to arctic Norway. We found some magnificent rock climbing on flawless granite but, when the weather deteriorated, decided to go and explore the Frostisen icecap. This was not a very sensible choice since low cloud stubbornly clung to its slopes throughout our visit. At one point we became disorientated and I was struggling to make sense of the map, an ancient relic that looked like nothing more than a sheet of paper covered in lots of dirty thumbprints.

I should have admitted that we were lost but I had a hunch as to where we might be. A momentary thinning of the cloud gave a veiled view of a large lake, far, far below but shining brightly through the gloom. Suddenly all seemed obvious – the map showed only one large lake anywhere nearby so we could only be on the slope above it. A descent to the lake and then down its out flowing river and we would be back at our base. Simple.

We set off. Some of the others did not share my confidence; the compass seemed to be pointing the wrong way and the gradient of the slope was unexpected but, despite these signals, I was unshakeable in my confidence that, at last, we were on the right track.

After about half an hour the lake seemed to loom larger through the mist, and indeed it was very large when we arrived there. Unfortunately, my 'lake' turned out to have actually been a snow patch. We were now properly lost but fortune sometimes smiles on the incompetent and, soon after, the mist lifted and we were able to trudge laboriously in the correct direction back to camp.

Psychologists recognise this widespread phenomenon of clinging to a particular opinion against all the evidence and call it 'confirmation bias'. I am a better navigator now but we should all recognise that confirmation bias lurks to lure the unwary leader into a trap of unwarranted confidence.

Self-made traps

There are plenty of other traps that arise from our attitudes or because we learn behaviour that contains an unidentified flaw. Over an extended period of involvement in an activity we learn to use rules of thumb as a reasonably accurate practical tool of decision-making. We rarely go systematically through every shred of relevant data, but, instead, use a time-tested but cruder process that operates on a model of reality rather than on reality itself. This has been called heuristic decision-making (McCammon, 2002).

Decisions rarely give us the time we would like to have to make them, so such an approach is a necessity in many situations. The problem arises at the points where our model of reality diverges importantly from reality itself.

An example of this is what is sometimes called 'negative event reinforcement', where unpunished violations of good practice persuade you that what you are doing is actually good behaviour. If you are a sailor who ignores the weather forecast for a few days or a few weeks without any adverse effect it is easy to think that you have moved onto some sort of higher plane where you no longer need the forecasts, where you can deal with anything that the sea can throw at you – until you get caught out.

In the 1980s a pair of alpine climbers pared down their clothing and equipment to a bare minimum, travelling super light and super fast, relying on their speed to avoid bad weather. They achieved astonishing times on their climbs until on an ascent of the North Face of the Piz Badile, a climb well within their capabilities, they were trapped by a sudden storm. Both climbers perished, their T-shirts and light jackets inadequate protection in a fierce summer thunderstorm.

When two girls drowned in a flooded river in the north of England during a river walking activity, it was found afterwards that a string of entirely uneventful previous visits by the same school had led to the assumption that the activity was not a hazardous one.

Everybody else knows best

A few ski tracks down a gully can completely shut down our critical faculties! As soon as other people start to do something that we have already rejected as unsafe or inappropriate, a strong pressure starts to work on us. Something unreasonable suddenly appears sensible. Skiing does portray this in especially clear terms because the use a slope has had is written on the snow. A gully rejected for its hazardous nature gets skied by some unknown person and suddenly, the rest of the world is queuing up to follow even if they know nothing of the competence of the pathfinder. You could find yourself following the tracks of a suicidal maniac but, because the tracks are there, someone else has in effect said 'It's OK' and your normal instincts are suppressed. This quirk is sometimes called 'social proof'.

It can be very difficult for leaders to go against the flow of social proof. If you are in charge of a group on a coastal walk and you want to control swimming in a bay that is known to have tricky tide rips, your task will be much the harder if you arrive to find dozens of children and dogs cavorting in the water.

How to make bad decisions

Groups don't always make the best decisions. Some research has suggested that group decision-making only works as a tool to make quality decisions because a group is more likely to contain a single individual who has the necessary expertise and really understands the situation. In most circumstances that single individual will make the best decisions, with groups tending only to achieve the least worst choice. There may be other benefits relating to motivation and morale that might make a group decision the right choice, but another of its problems is the observation that groups tend to make more risky decisions than would their individual members. In the tradition of the elaborate names that are used to describe these important phenomena, this is sometimes called the 'group risk shift phenomenon'.

Supply and demand

Scarcity is as important in adventure activities as it is in the operation of a commercial market. You are much less likely to make the right decision on the day if you know you are not going to get a second chance. Bank holidays and blue skies tend to coincide rarely, in Britain at least, so when they happen, people fortunate enough to be on the sea, on rivers and on mountains tend to make some shaky decisions just to seize the opportunity.

Supervision

There are some generic issues that apply to virtually all activities from simple walks just outside school through to challenging multi-day expeditions. At a layer below the broad sweep of leadership are the immediate demands of active supervision. Lapses in hands-on supervision are regularly a primary or contributory cause of serious incidents, so focusing our attention on supervision can be highly productive.

At its most fundamental we expect the leader's supervision to monitor the performance and well-being of each individual engaged in the activity. This is the raw data on which most safety and quality-related decisions will be made so, except in the special case of unaccompanied activity, its constant collection is vital. We can only modify the difficulty or intensity of an activity to match what an individual child requires if we have been alert to the performance of that particular child through active watching, listening and questioning.

Focus

Instructors should guard against focusing an undue amount of their attention on one person at the expense of another. A person in difficulty, of course, requires personal attention, but it is often a mistake to assume that others are not having similar difficulties, perhaps in a less immediately apparent way. In any given group there may be individuals with whom the instructor has a particular rapport and those with whom he has none. Each has equal rights to proper supervision centred on them as individuals. Some people manifest their anxiety about the activity in uncooperative behaviour and leaders must try to rise above confrontation that only makes the situation worse.

Although supervision should be most evident at an individual level there is also a need for the leader to be aware and informed at a group level.

Supervision in practice

Success in adventure activities is often characterised as the art of being in the right place at the right time. This is certainly a great asset to the leader's ability to supervise. The effective leader is not usually to be found striding out 50 metres ahead of the group, or showing his awesome speed on a cycle descent, but instead is in among the group to gauge the progress of each individual. During a journey the leader will often see more and learn more in the middle or at the back of the party.

A simple improvised game. The instructors are close enough to intervene if necessary. Some may choose to use helmets in this situation.

When technical work is being done at a more static location positioning remains critical. It is all too easy for the instructor to stand where crucial details are obscured from view and where intervention in the event of a problem is awkward. Far better to stand where the main hazards are in view, where the participants most exposed to the hazard are also in view and in sufficiently close proximity that the instructor can readily give support or actively intervene.

Sometimes, defining 'no go' areas can be useful and some instructors use a length of rope or a piece of hazard tape to mark out the limits. Positioning oneself between the pupil and the hazard can be a good place for the instructor to be.

Ratio

The supervisory ratio between leaders and led is important. When guides lead an ascent of the Matterhorn they do so with a ratio of 1 : 1 – a guide for every client – but when making a journey on the glacier a short distance away, the ratio might be 1 : 6, because the terrain is less technically demanding. A walk with adults in simple countryside terrain may be perfectly reasonable with a ratio of 1 : 16 yet the same walk undertaken with children who display very challenging behaviour might need 1 : 4 or less.

Making the decision as to the appropriate ratio is a key responsibility of providers and leaders. Although, it will often be convenient to have a standard operating ratio for a particular activity there needs to be sufficient flexibility in the arrangements to deal with varying demands. Many governing bodies avoid giving a 'recommended ratio' because of the variability of circumstances and corresponding demands on the leader. Some of the guidance to schools from the Scottish Executive suggests possible ratios as follows:

- 1 adult to 15–20 group members for excursions where the element of risk to be encountered is similar to that normally encountered in daily life, e.g. excursions to sites of historic interest, most field work, local walks, etc.

- 1 adult to 10 group members for all trips abroad.

- Within each of these categories, schools may want to consider, for example for children under the age of 8 or for children with additional support needs, whether a lower ratio, of 1 adult to 6 (or fewer) group members should apply.

- For higher risk activities, consideration will need to be given to greater adult supervision, as appropriate.

(Scottish Executive, 2005)

Tight ratios of leaders to participants are likely to be needed when:

- the activity is technically demanding;

- direct intervention by an instructor is likely to be needed at an individual level;

- errors by participants may have serious consequences;

- participants may have difficulty in understanding or acting upon instructions.

Looser ratios of leaders to participants may be acceptable when:

- the activity does not make high technical demands on learners;

- errors by participants are easily avoided or not likely to be serious in nature;

- participants are expected to be able to follow instructions;

- participants are already experienced in the activity.

Assistant leaders

The presence of an assistant leader has a great deal to commend it except in the most straightforward undertakings. As in so many other situations, the test for the appropriate level of supervision is to ask what would happen if:

- several people capsized/fell/got into difficulties at the same time?

- someone made a serious technical error like an unfastened harness?

- a participant collapsed?

- the leader collapsed?

- the weather suddenly became severe?

and so on. Of course, the very worst reason for a poor ratio is that no more supervisory staff were available … In that situation, radical modification of plans or abandonment are to be considered.

Scrambling in an exposed location on the Skye Ridge. A difficult supervisory exercise for the instructor.

Adult assistants

With some groups, particularly those of young people, the supervisory ratio can be improved by the presence of responsible adult assistants, often volunteers or interested parents. Although not qualified as leaders in the activity, such people can provide a valuable extra pair of hands to the leader and can be a great asset if someone needs to go for help or if a child is to curtail their involvement in the activity. However, the limitations of such assistance must be kept in view. The leader must beware of assuming a level of technical knowledge that may not exist in the assistant, must be ready to give guidance and direction, and must be in no doubt that, they, the leader, retain overall responsibility. Volunteer leaders of this kind should not usually be left in charge except when an appropriate emergency response demands it.

Residential programmes often require 24-hour supervision of participants. Although not all of this time will involve students doing outdoor activities, pastoral care and supervision is certainly needed during down time. When professional instructors provide the primary supervision of activities, out-of-hours supervision and pastoral care may be agreed as a responsibility of visiting teachers under the umbrella of the provider's night-duty arrangements.

Who is in charge?

When any group has multiple leaders or instructors it is undesirable for there to be any ambiguity about who is in charge. It is not uncommon for parties under joint leadership to get into difficulties because each leader assumes that the other will make the difficult decision to turn back or change plan, with the result that necessary action is not taken.

Allocation of other roles should be considered, including the appointment of a back marker or 'tail end Charlie' If navigational difficulties are encountered on a journey it is all too easy for the leader to be drawn into paying maximum attention to the map and minimum attention to the group and its members. If an assistant has sufficient skill, a delegation of the navigation function will make it easier for a leader to take the overview so necessary to good leadership and group management.

Head count

The head count is a basic tool of the leader, a simple idea but one that can be difficult to apply in practice. The supervisory span of a single leader is limited and becomes more so in irregular terrain or with volatile groups. 'Like herding cats' is how one leader described the process to me. Head counts are worthwhile whenever there is a halt or change of situation such as embarking or disembarking from vehicles, or simply if one of the supervisors has a feeling of uncertainty. 'Now, I haven't seen Pete for a few minutes …'

An important technique is to subdivide larger groups into smaller, each allocated to the supervision of an identified leader or assistant. This puts the head count within the span of attention of each leader and ensures that each child is under direct supervision from a responsible adult.

Jonathan Attwell, aged 10 years, died tragically on 16 October 1999 during a walking expedition on Snowdon when he became separated from a large group of older boys and leaders and fell from the cliffs of Clogwyn y Garnedd. The party had become strung out on steep broken ground on the East Ridge and his absence went unnoticed for a long period until the party regrouped. Perhaps the most tragic aspect was that the group had a good overall ratio, with four leaders to twelve children, but since no subdivision into smaller units had taken place it seems likely that no individual leader felt that they had immediate supervisory responsibility for Jonathan rather than a more general overseeing role.

Unaccompanied journeys

A skilful leader can give his or her group a fantastic experience of adventure activities and much of this book is concerned with how we should take on this primary task. However, an imaginative leader will consciously flex the level of supervision and control that exists between leader and group in order to maximise the educational benefit. Beginners, anxious individuals or young children may need very close supervision and shoulder-to-shoulder encouragement from the leader; more confident participants, who perhaps already have a few days' experience of the activity, may usefully be given a longer leash. There is an added intensity to the experience when the instructor hands over real responsibility to participants and the lessons of self-reliance and self-confidence are likely to come thick and fast in such situations.

> To lead people, walk beside them. As for the best leaders, the people do not notice their existence. The next best, the people honour and praise. The next, the people fear; and the next, the people hate. When the best leader's work is done the people say, 'We did it ourselves!'

Lao Tsu's famous remark suggests that the pinnacle of leadership lies in the unaccompanied journey, where the leader supports and prepares the members of the group to go it alone to their own great benefit. In organised adventure activities, an important element of control will usually remain with the leader together with an overall moral and practical responsibility. The leader in such a situation is often exercising what is called 'remote supervision'. It is not an easy thing to lead a group at any time. When remote supervision takes place, the responsible person is not travelling with the group but giving 'supervision at a distance'. The method is most commonly used for expeditions on foot but similar principles would apply in other disciplines.

Remote supervision

To be effective, remote supervision will usually depend upon:

- a competent and experienced supervisor familiar with the route and the terrain;
- a group of an appropriate number, who are well trained and appropriately equipped;
- the presence of suitable leadership within the group;
- a suitable and well practised emergency plan and method of emergency contact;
- a route that has been carefully chosen to reflect the abilities of the group and the expected conditions;
- an understanding between supervisor and group of the level of supervision that will be in place;
- arrangements for monitoring through occasional contact by telephone, by written messages or direct rendezvous;
- a thorough risk assessment of the plans.

Remote supervision is challenging and needs experience, imagination and sound judgement in the supervisor. While certain NGB awards indicate a valuable level of competence as a leader in the activity, few of them specifically cover remote supervision. A qualification to lead in the terrain in question would normally be considered a good starting point for the remote supervisor but nobody should ignore the greater inherent difficulties that the supervisor will face and the need for a careful approach.

There is a progression in remote supervision which starts with 'shadowing' where the supervisor follows the group at a distance and then extends to methods that use intermittent, usually prearranged, contact.

There is a danger that shadowing gives both group and supervisor an impression of a greater level of safety than actually exists. Some emergencies can arise unexpectedly and then develop with dizzying speed. If the supervisor is sufficiently remote from the group to give them a proper sense of independence, it may take several minutes to join the main party in the event of difficulties. The degree of separation is crucial.

Choice of route for remotely supervised groups

In my opinion, the group should be on a route where their training will enable them to be self-sufficient in all eventualities, with checks providing an additional safety net. It is not acceptable for a group to be on a route that is too difficult for them, or to be travelling in unsuitable conditions, simply because a supervisor hopes to be able to keep an eye on them and to intervene in the event of problems. If the leader is not certain that the group are well prepared, well equipped and on a route suitable for their competence, then an alternative approach with greater control, such as a led walk, should be given serious consideration.

A tragic occurrence in the Scottish Highlands found a 'shadowed' group of young adults attempting to cross a swollen river in heavy rain and high winds. The supervisor saw this happening and tried to prevent the crossing, but his shouts were not heard and by the time he could run to join the group, one of the party had drowned.

A suitable route will usually be of a lesser difficulty and degree of challenge than that which a skilled leader could expect to undertake with the same group – there needs to be a margin of safety to allow the inevitable making of errors by the group. Choice of route is one of the strongest controls that the leader possesses. The alternatives of a Plan A and Plan B are desirable throughout and groups should have been given some insight into when and how plans might be changed.

Contact and communication

Mobile telephone calls or text messages are probably the most convenient method of remote contact but may be unreliable due to obstructed signals (common in mountain terrain) or flat batteries. In addition, the ability to phone the outside world to chat or for specific advice tends to shatter the illusion of remoteness and self-sufficiency, so that a number of organisations have adopted a policy of sealing phones for emergency use only. Routeing the group past telephone boxes can be a more reliable alternative in some cases – cash or a phone card will normally be necessary.

Traditionally, walking groups would leave messages such as note in a film canister in a cairn, or in a plastic bag attached to a prominent tree, but these can be an unwelcome intrusion into wild places. Modern tracking technology by satellite may make it possible to monitor the position of a group at all times (barring technical problems) but this only tells the supervisor where the transmitter is, not what might be happening.

Direct contact between supervisor and group, where the supervisor drops in to pay a visit, sounds simple but in wild country can be surprisingly problematical. A pre-arranged rendezvous at a fixed point is generally reliable but if the group are travelling fast they can be forced into a cold and tedious wait for the supervisor; if slow they may miss the rendezvous, or worse, shortcut safe operation to catch up on lost time.

Far better from the group's point of view is for the supervisor to find them, but this can be frustratingly difficult, and especially so in poor visibility. If travelling on a linear feature such as a footpath, the supervisor walking the reciprocal route is to be recommended as an effective approach.

It is useful for the supervisor to carry binoculars to confirm a sighting of the correct group. It should be recognised that if a supervisor is working alone, there is an increased threat to their own safety. If an accompanying assistant is not available then an appropriate lone-working policy should be adopted. It is normal for one supervisor to supervise a single group in order to be able to give the necessary undivided attention but an experienced supervisor may, under carefully assessed circumstances and in familiar terrain, supervise several groups

A high level of familiarity with the terrain and route is desirable so that the supervisor can make informed speculation as to where a group might be at a given time and where are the likely areas of difficulty. Except in the most simple terrain, map knowledge alone is likely to be insufficient.

Similarly, hands-on personal knowledge of the group and its training is highly desirable. In its absence, care should be taken to meet the group and, if possible, their trainer in order to establish a good understanding of their competence and likely style of operation.

One of the greatest difficulties for supervisors, and one generating many anxious hours, is to decide what to do when expected contact has not been made. Experience tells us that the group is almost certainly fit and well, having simply missed the rendezvous, but there is usually an underlying concern that they just may be in grave difficulty. Missing a single check usually encourages us to send someone to try to get sight of the group; missing two consecutive checks is taken very seriously.

Progression to independence

On longer courses, or through extended periods of session-by-session contact, there can be a progressive handover of responsibility to participants and a stepping back of the instructor. The model followed during sixty years of classic Outward Bound® courses, which are of three- or four-week duration, can be seen in the following example for a hill based programme:

- *Phase One*. The instructor trains and coaches the group in key technical skills such as navigation, map reading and campcraft and a number of mountain journeys of progressively increasing difficulty are tackled The issues of leadership and group interaction are explored using additional activities.

- *Phase Two*. The group undertake mountain journeys where they take primary responsibility for planning and execution. The instructor is present and may give some additional coaching but is mainly seen as a source of technical information and as a safety officer who will intervene if things begin to go awry.

- *Phase Three*. The group plan mountain journeys to be undertaken without the instructor being present. Initially this will be a single-day ascent but will usually culminate in an unaccompanied mountain expedition of three days' duration. The instructor has to approve the choice of route and the quality of the planning.

The expedition section of the Duke of Edinburgh's Award is heavily dependent on remote supervision of the groups taking part. This is done by volunteer supervisors and assessors. Schemes for the training and accreditation of assessors and supervisors have been developed. The supervisor represents the Operating Authority (the body authorised to operate the Award) and is ultimately responsible for safety. The assessor ensures that the necessary conditions are met and, as someone with considerable local knowledge, advises on safety. The assessor will be a member of a local Wild Country Panel who oversee, screen and advise Award expeditions in their particular area. The supervisor is expected to have in-depth knowledge of the group and their previous training, including practice expeditions. Groups will be of 4–7 young people and, for Gold expeditions, will make a four-day expedition or exploration involving at least eight hours of planned, purposeful activity each day.

Any organisation that allows unaccompanied ventures to take place will know that things can and do go wrong. A relative beginner cannot be expected to have the judgemental or navigational skills of an old hand, so mistakes will inevitably occur. Planning should reflect this. Sometimes internal conflict within the group has a disruptive effect and splits can occur or arguments develop. As with any journey in wild country, the unexpected can occur and no group is immune from the possibility of illness.

Although things do go wrong, experienced providers have developed systems that have stood the test of time and which usually prevent considerable difficulties becoming crises.

Above all, it should be recognised that huge benefits accrue to those taking part in unaccompanied ventures. When I was Principal at Outward Bound® Eskdale, I made a point of meeting groups after their return from the 'final' expedition, a journey of thirty miles or more through the Lakeland fells. Nobody could listen to the enthusiastic and heartfelt accounts of the 17 and 18 year olds without being certain that they had just been through a genuinely life-enhancing experience that they would never forget – a true rite of passage.

Chapter summary

- Pattern recognition is a key skill developed primarily through experience.
- Commonly occurring patterns that contribute to accidents include:
    - trying to please other people;
    - being blinded by the prize;
    - failing to see the whole picture;
    - perceived time pressure.
- Leaders often feel themselves to be invulnerable – they are not!
- Leaders should be aware of the positive and negative effects on the quality of their judgement.
- Accidents happen when weaknesses in our defences 'line up'.
- Self-made traps arise from our own distorted perception – few of us are immune.
- The quality of immediate supervision has a strong effect on safety.
- Unaccompanied journeys are one of the highest expressions of adventure education but need special management.

Chapter 9

Parents

'Better drowned than duffers – if not duffers, won't drown' (*Swallows and Amazons*, Arthur Ransome).

Keeping the benefits in view

If I can be forgiven some evangelism I would like to make it absolutely clear that, in my view, giving your children the opportunity to engage with outdoor adventure is one of the best things you can do for them.

Nobody can argue that outdoor activities are without risk. It is too easy to assume that the rest of life is risk free but, of course, this is mistaken. Risk is part of life and especially part of growing up. No parent can completely protect their child against risk, nor should we succumb to the temptation to attempt to do so. Perhaps the most that we, as parents, can hope to do is to help to steer our children in directions where there is the best chance of growth and positive development.

Arthur Ransome brilliantly captured the essence of childhood adventure in his superb *Swallows and Amazons* books, which have transcended their origins in a different age and a distant class to remain inspirational today. At the start of the first book in the series, the four children ask permission to take their dinghy *Swallow* on an extended lake expedition to Wild Cat Island without the encumbrance of adults. The final decision lies with Commander Walker, the children's father and a naval officer serving abroad. A telegram arrives. The quotation at the head of this chapter is the Commander's enigmatic reply. The children eventually work out that it means 'Yes' and a fantastic adventure starts to unroll. How many of us would be so imaginative in our reaction to the bold proposals of 21st-century children?

That suicide is a major cause of death among young adult males gives us a chilling picture of empty, frustrated lives. Use of the most dangerous drugs is surely a signal of a person seeking escape from emptiness and a lack of purpose and inspiration. Adventure activities are no panacea but they do give opportunities – many would say unrivalled opportunities – for expressing the self through action, for giving a sense of being part of nature, for co-operation, for the growth of confidence and identity and for the intense peak experiences that make life precious.

Even the occasional child who feels no affinity with the outdoors will have had an experi-ence to remember, a taste of wild places and a sense that the much vaunted 'environment' that extends deeper and further than keeping litter off the streets.

Adventure is both personal and relative. It is not necessary to sail the Atlantic in order to have a memorable outdoor experience. If you have never seen a herd of cows, a visit to the countryside can be a revelation; if you have never been out of the city, a dark night sky stud-ded with stars, unforgettable. I will never forget the first night that, as a boy, I slept out in the open on a nondescript hillside in Derbyshire, although in truth I was so excited that little sleep transpired. Landscape, adventure, fun and a sense of doing something special and unique to me all combined into a great experience that is still with me when almost all my classroom lessons have receded into the mists.

How can anyone deny their kids that! TV is no substitute for reality!

What to expect from providers

Information

The parent or guardian of anyone under 18 years of age is normally expected to give con-sent for their child to take part in out-of-school activities such as adventure activities, residential stays and visits abroad. Parents should expect to be properly informed as to:

- when and where the visit is planned to take place;
- the objectives of the visit;
- the travel arrangements, including the timetable and rendezvous for departure and return;
- the size of group and the nature of supervision, including the names of supervising staff or assistants;
- arrangements for dealing with special educational needs, medical conditions and illnesses;
- expected standards of behaviour, including, where applicable, alcohol, sexual behaviour and prohibited substances;
- what clothing, other items or money the child should bring;
- what insurance is in place or is expected to be arranged by parents;
- any payment to be made;
- emergency contact details for participants.

It is particularly important that parents are given an accurate understanding of what is planned. In adventure activities, there have been a number of cases where parents have been given information by the leader that has failed to give an accurate picture of what the child will really be involved in. See Chapter 14 for more on this.

For example, the leader's view of 'walking' may extend to exposed and rocky mountain ridges; the parent may expect the activity thus described to be confined to signposted country paths. This degree of confusion helps nobody, and in the event of accident leads to recrimination. Parents have a right to know what the plan really entails.

How to select a provider

There is a wide variety of adventure experience available for school parties. When activities are offered that are in scope for AALA, then an AALA licence is mandatory for courses or other events being offered to those under 18 years. See Chapter 7 for more on this. The AALA licence therefore represents an indicator of a standard of provision that can be judged to meet acceptable standards of operation.

Private clients can be similarly reassured when an AALA licence is held. For outdoor experiences targeted at adults, no licencing is necessary, but some providers who work both with adults and children may hold the licence anyway and this is a positive signal for the buyer of services.

More difficult is the position when a provider is not required to hold a licence – because all their activities are out of scope. Adult-only providers or voluntary organisations are examples.

Assessing the quality and safety of such providers needs a more investigative approach. Most operate to high standards, but, as in any field, there can be wide variations. Many subscribe to non-statutory schemes of accreditation operated by particular groupings of providers. BAHA – the British Activity Holidays Association – is an example. When a provider is part of an accreditation scheme it is wise to confirm that the scheme does include some form of accreditation of safe operation and is not simply a badge of membership.

If the provider cannot offer convincing accreditation, or you need further reassurance, it can be useful to ask some of the following questions to help you to reach a sensible decision:

- How do you train and authorise leaders?
- Do leaders hold NGB awards?
- How long have you been in business?
- What happens to people who have difficulties with the activity?
- What is your safety record like?
- Who will oversee the individual leaders and how?
- Is there anybody who can give me a reference?

It is worth remembering that travel to and from the venue may be at least as hazardous as the activities to be offered when you get there.

I would have little confidence in providers that deny ever having accidents or who are unwilling to answer questions like these. Some providers will automatically give you an indication of their approach to risk and ask you to acknowledge that some risk is present (see Chapter 14). This is usually a positive indicator of an organisation that takes its responsibilities seriously.

If you choose a provider who is not licenced or part of any accreditation scheme, or does not have the back up of a large organisation, you need to have confidence in your own judgement in making the choice. As in so many situations in life there are no definite answers and *caveat emptor* must be the ruling principle.

Freelance providers

If, as a beginner or the parent of a beginner, you ignore larger organisations and put yourself in the charge of an individual instructor or volunteer, you expect that person to understand how to teach efficiently, choose the correct equipment, manage the main hazards, know what to do in an emergency and so on. There are some brilliant leaders in this sector together with a few who are distinctly shaky. So how do you decide who is suitable?

It is best to look for NGB qualifications (see Chapter 3) and substantial experience. You might phone him and be told 'I've been doing this for years – since when there were just a handful of us. Hundreds of students and no accidents. You'll love it!' When you ask if he is qualified, he tells you that he was part of the group that set up the qualification structure years ago but he could never be bothered to get the ticket; 'You know how it is – I'd rather be out there in the fresh air than attending a boring lecture!'

If you are a cautious person you may already have heard enough to persuade you that this is just a little too casual for your taste, but if you are more of a risk taker you may already be intrigued by the prospect of learning with one of the all time greats of the sport – like being taught to play golf by Arnold Palmer. *Caveat emptor* indeed!

Some would-be leaders or providers complain that unreasonable demands for qualifications or training are placed upon them and that this destroys spontaneity. To a degree they may have a point. However, in his 2006 Reith Lectures, Daniel Barenboim said, in the context of music education: 'The more you know, the freer you are.' In my opinion, this argument can be transferred to our own area. Usually, the best prepared, trained, qualified and experienced leaders are the ones best able to give high-quality outdoor adventure.

Information from you

It is an encouraging sign if the provider wants to find out from you information that will improve their ability to manage risks. This might include:

- information on medical conditions, allergies, medication, disabilities;
- ability to swim or level of water confidence;
- any recent injuries or illnesses;
- contact details of next of kin;
- contact details of doctor.

You may be asked to give authorisation for emergency medical treatment in the unlikely event that this proves necessary.

The deep end

For youngsters on programmes of outdoor education the risks appear to be very similar to those in the classroom – small indeed but not invisible. However, a small number of young adults graduate from adventure education to personal participation in adventure sports at a high level and, as is the case with young drivers, there will often be a period when capability outruns any underlying capacity for sound judgement. Risks (and, it must be said, rewards too) can be at a relatively high level until the powerful instinct for self-preservation reasserts itself. Having your 14 year old daughter leading poorly protected rock climbs with great *sang froid* or doing hazardous aerial manoeuvres on skis with aplomb would fill most parents with a mixture of deep pride and deep apprehension – the essence of parenthood perhaps.

Chapter summary

- AALA licensing is a good indicator of safe operation in providers.
- Many good providers may fall out of scope of the licencing regulations. Alternative accreditation or other evidence should be sought from these.
- What information a provider gives the client (or, for minors, their parent) and expects from the client signals the quality of operation.

Chapter 10

The activities

Activities are at the core of outdoor education and anyone involved as leader or manager is likely to have in-depth knowledge of at least one or two and passing knowledge of others. This chapter aims to give a tour of some of the main activities, to identify some of the common problem areas in each of them. This is only done for the most prominent and widely used activities and is intended to provide an overview for non-specialists, not a substitute for proper direct experience and the advice of national governing bodies (NGBs). The general principles will apply to all activities.

Variety of activities

The provision of outdoor education is much wider than that provided by residential outdoor centres, and extends far beyond the recognised adventure sports, but the results of a survey of outdoor centres in 1999 by the Health and Safety Laboratory gives a useful breakdown of the activities offered by about a hundred such centres. The list given in Table 10.1, which is derived from that survey, indicates the percentage of the total number of centres offering each activity and also lists them in rank order by the number of participant hours. Thus we see that 71 per cent of all centres offer trekking (walking) of some kind, and that this activity has seen the greatest number of participant hours.

There are difficulties in applying consistent criteria when comparing different activities and different providers but it is certainly clear that the most commonly offered and most commonly taken up activities are trekking, paddle sports and climbing, with a second tier of less widely used but still prominent activities such as sailing, gorge scrambling, rafting and mountain biking.

Table 10.1 Percentage of centres offering activities

	% of total offering	Rank order of participant hours for each activity	
Canoeing	71	4	
Trekking	71	1	(highest)
Climbing	69	2	
Kayaking	68	3	
Gorge scrambling	52	7	
Mountain biking	46	10	
Sailing	42	6	
Rafting	34	11	
Caving	32	8	
Windsurfing	26	9	
Skiing	18	5	
Orienteering	16	12	

National governing bodies

NGBs are the bodies that promote, represent and control the activities in their ambit and as such are an essential source of information on good practice, on what can go wrong, and how. Information on adverse occurrences allows one to learn vicariously from the experiences of others.

In Britain, the British Canoe Union (BCU), the Royal Yachting Association (RYA) and the British Mountaineering Council (BMC) are all examples of NGBs. Some sports and activities have more than one body that aspire to representation and some separate the coaching or leadership function, which may be of a professional nature, from amateur participation.

All will have means to support and disseminate good practice and, most will have a system for the training and qualification of instructors and leaders. This makes NGBs an invaluable source of information and advice on current issues for participants in the sport and especially for both volunteer and professional leaders.

Some NGBs, particularly the larger ones, can provide advice of a highly specialist nature. So we find that the BMC has a Technical Committee that looks at equipment failure, the RYA advises on how marine regulation and safety issues impacts on individual sailors and the BCU has information on sport-specific issues such as the occurrence of a particular injury when kayakers roll. One imagines that the BCU will also have a particular concern with current issues.

Other bodies

Although NGBs are the fount of knowledge on their own activities, voluntary organisations such as the Duke of Edinburgh's Award or the Scout Association and professional bodies such as the Institute for Outdoor Learning or trade associations like the British Activity Holidays Association can all give helpful guidance on the delivery of activities in a particular context.

Primary cause

Although it is impossible to detail every mechanism, in this chapter I have attempted to collect some of the more frequent scenarios that lead to adverse events in the various activities, so that leaders and providers can test the relevance of existing arrangements against these known problems of regular occurrence.

I am grateful to the Outward Bound® Trust for allowing me to compile information from their incident database – which now covers well over one million activity days – and also for the Trust's admirable openness about safety issues. I should point out that most of the incidents described below did not originate with that organisation. The Outward Bound® incident database routinely classifies the primary cause of incidents under one (one only – the prime cause) of the following headings, a fairly crude but nevertheless informative process:

Alcohol	Drugs	Fall/slip
Avalanche	Equipment	Fall on rock
Clothing	Exceeded ability	Fall on snow
Capsize	Exhaustion	Falling rock
Darkness	Failed to follow	Fast water
Dehydration	instructions	Hazardous animal
Intruder	Misbehaviour	Technique
Immersion	Missing/lost	Unfit
Instruction	Overboard	Weather
Lightning	Psychological	Other
Medication	Supervision	

Although this list resembles one of those party games where players have to assemble an arbitrary collection of words into a story, this list is remarkably all embracing, with use of the 'other' category a relatively infrequent necessity. You have possibly guessed that the most frequent cause in general adventure activities is 'Fall/slip'. Some of the categories occur infrequently. In the UK, 'Hazardous animal' is rarely cited but the occasional adder incident keeps it in the list. In the international sphere, we may find 'Aggressive behaviour by elephant' as a more exotic example of an occurrence of a hazardous animal.

The pattern of incidents by primary cause is likely to vary considerably between different providers, different activities and different regions but, for a particular provider, one would often find similar, recurrent patterns of occurrence from year to year.

I should emphasise that adventure activities are far from being as dangerous as this list of 'what can go wrong' might suggest. A competent leader will be aware that, for instance, the hazard of drowning is ever present in a canoe session but we hope that they will manage things in a manner that maintains the risk at a vanishingly small level. Knowing a hazard exists, or that a particular combination of circumstances has led to disaster in the past forearms us to prevent its reoccurrence.

All activities

Critical safety equipment

An essential practical aspect of supervision in many activities is the routine fitting and checking of safety equipment. Instructors, in their desire to move quickly to the exciting content of the session, cannot afford to overlook this.

Many items of critical safety equipment need to be properly and securely fitted if they are to give the required protection. These checks are of the highest importance and experienced instructors will have developed a routine to get this done to a high standard every time. Newer instructors do not always register the vital importance of doing simple but essential things with complete reliability.

Helmets can only give effective protection if, at the first impact, the shell of the helmet stays in place. A poorly fitted helmet can also slip off the head so that the straps and harness become agents of strangulation. It is wise to give a careful briefing on helmet fitting and check the result, concluding with a simulated glancing blow from the checker's hand. A well fitted helmet stays on the head through this check.

Personal flotation devices (PFDs) will float in most situations. The trick is to ensure that the person wearing it stays firmly attached and supported above the water – not suspended some way beneath. This is such a vital component of protection that every fitted PFD should be checked by a responsible person.

Climbing harnesses must be snugly fitted and the process needs careful attention at all times. Sit harnesses are the most commonly used. When both leg loops and waist belt are adjustable a better fit is usually achieved if the legs are loosened off and not retightened until after the waist belt is tightened snugly (typically to the point where two fingers can, with difficulty, be inserted inside the belt). Fitting demands particular care when bulky clothing is worn or when the subject does not have a clearly defined waist. In that case it can be desirable to use an additional chest harness to prevent the subject slipping out of the harness in the event of an inverted fall.

Many climbing harnesses have buckles that are only secure if 'doubled back'. It is by no means infrequent for even experienced climbers to set off without this essential precaution – and people have lost their lives as a result. There is no alternative to careful checks by the instructor and by peers in a 'buddy system'. Checkers should be alert to the fact that wearers may have adjusted the harness since the time that it was fitted, to change clothing or for a toilet break.

Unaccompanied journeys

Adventure activities unaccompanied by instructors are brilliant learning experiences for everyone and most especially for children and young adults. Some activities, such as orienteering, where youngsters navigate alone or in small groups through mapped woodland, can give a flavour of independent operation but the full manifestation seems to come most readily from overland journeys and expeditions in open canoes. Imagine the satisfaction of a small group of 17 year olds who have travelled for four days through a mountain landscape or down a great river, camping and cooking, planning and dealing with the unexpected, alone and self-sufficient except for a bare minimum of adult contact. Instructors wax eloquent about the joys of self-reliance and self-discovery but are perhaps too ready to get in the way of a deep learning experience by taking unnecessarily close control of it. See Chapter 8 for more.

Water activities

The main problem with water activities is the water. It is an ever present background, which, of course, adds much of the joy and character of water sports but it is also the origin of the ever-present threats of drowning and, in most climates, hypothermia.

Personal flotation

Drowning in adventure activities should normally be a hazard easily addressed by the use of personal buoyancy. Although things are rarely quite that simple, well fitting personal flotation is *de rigueur* for most water activities. Drowning tends to occur when no buoyancy is worn (through neglect or intentionally, as might be the case in swimming or some combined water rock situations), when there is some powerful influence that overcomes the effect of the flotation (such as being physically trapped under a tree branch or a flooded cave passage) or when some other influence such as hypothermia is dominant.

Leaders should be familiar with the physiological aspects of drowning, the existence of 'dry drowning' and the different effects of fresh and salt water. Secondary drowning is of particular concern since it can result in the death of a person two or three days after an apparently successful rescue.

Personal flotation devices exist in a huge range of designs and specifications. Any reputable manufacturer will publish a summary of the different specifications and indicate their suitability for particular applications. Typical provision would include a 50 Newton buoyancy aid and life jackets of 100, 150 and 275 Newtons. The figure 50 Newton (50 N) is a measure of the uplift force provided by the flotation device and is equivalent to about 5.5 kg of uplift.

One of the key messages is that only a high-specification life jacket can give protection to an unconscious person by preventing them from floating face down. Buoyancy aids give vital extra buoyancy to a person able to help him or herself but will not be suitable if the victim has been knocked unconscious or has succumbed to hypothermia to a point where they have lost the ability to control their posture in the water. One manufacturer gives the following advice on the use of a 50 N buoyancy aid:

- Only suitable for competent swimmers.

- For sheltered water use where help is close at hand.

- Only provides support to a conscious person who can help themselves.

Many people in physically demanding sports such as river kayaking prefer a snug-fitting buoyancy aid to a life jacket on the grounds that it keeps them warmer, gives all-round protection to the torso from impacts, such as being struck by the bow of a kayak, and does not obstruct their agility and freedom of movement. In the final analysis, if out of the boat and swimming, the protection against drowning may be greater with an inflated life jacket but the paddler's ability to avoid the capsize in the first place is probably greater with the buoyancy aid.

By contrast, if someone falls overboard in a storm from an offshore sailing cruiser, the situation is immediately grave and extended immersion is likely. A life jacket with a high level of flotation is essential to keep the wearer's face out of the water and to float them high in the aerated water of breaking waves. Face protection against spray is desirable.

Buoyancy aids are a good choice for parties under instruction when:

- the situation is confined to a limited area;

- rescue is likely to be simple and rapid;

- the wearer has good water confidence;

- extreme conditions are considered to be unlikely.

Life jackets may be preferable when:

- the area of operation is unconfined;

- rescue may be problematic with possible extended immersion;

- the wearer has poor water confidence;

- extreme conditions may be encountered.

In general, the more extreme the situation, the more desirable is the protection of extra buoyancy over the 50 N minimum. Life jackets will usually have an attached whistle for drawing attention and in severe situations may also have an integral strobe light. Some are inflated by gas canisters, some by mouth.

When an appropriate PFD has been selected it must be a proper fit to the wearer if it is to give good protection. If extended immersion is a possibility, some arrangement of leg loop or crutch strap can prevent the person slumping too low in the floating aid.

Clothing and immersion hypothermia

Most water sports carry some risk of immersion in cold water, and some involve more or less permanent immersion. At lower water temperatures it is desirable to have protection against heat loss on immersion, except when immersion is certain to be brief. Because of the increased cooling effect of cold water, the onset of hypothermia can be much more rapid than in, say, mountain hypothermia.

A well equipped dinghy sailor.

Standard statistics indicate that for immersion in the temperature range 4–10 °C an adult will succumb to exhaustion or unconsciousness in 30–60 minutes and will die within 1–3 hours. The ability to swim or act rationally is likely to be lost even before the onset of exhaustion, especially if panic also occurs.

In very cold water, a fit capable adult can be reduced to helplessness or worse in a few minutes. A child of smaller body mass loses heat more rapidly and so in these circumstances would fare much worse than an adult, with a shorter period before the onset of a significant deterioration.

Wet suits – which trap a thin layer of water under an insulating layer of neoprene – and dry suits – which provide a fully waterproof barrier outside of a layer of insulating clothing – are the usual choices. The circumstances will determine when protective clothing is desirable, but some providers use a water temperature of 10 degrees Celcius as a guide.

Dinghy sailing

Clearly, the level of hazard in dinghy sailing is closely related to the operating environment. Sheltered inland waters escape many of the challenges to be found in exposed coastal waters. Off the coast it may be necessary to be equipped with an anchor, flares, navigational aids and radio communication. Such things would not normally be considered necessary in sheltered inland waters. A well found craft is essential in any situation. Bailers and paddles or oars are necessary except in special circumstances.

When dinghy sailing is taught in sailing schools there is usually some provision of a rescue craft or safety boat. Driving that craft is a skilled task and executing a rescue safely is even more so. The combination of swimmers in the water and a rotating propeller is not a comfortable one, and assisting an inverted craft needs prompt and focused action. The person in charge of the rescue boat needs training and experience appropriate to these challenges. Safety management should rarely be entirely dependent on the intervention of a safety boat – engine breakdown or propeller entanglement with weed, debris or loose fishing gear can suddenly disable the rescue boat when it is most needed.

Capsizes are commonplace and are usually without undue hazard but very infrequently one of the crew may be trapped, perhaps by entanglement with the rigging or other equipment. Although there is likely to be an accumulation of air under the upturned hull, a trapped person may be held with their head under the water – a serious emergency. Training in capsize drill, care to eliminate possible trapping hazards and prompt intervention by a safety boat crew will all address these hazards. Some teaching craft have masthead floats that prevent full inversion. It is traditional for sailors to carry knives to cut free entanglements. Leaders should ensure that everybody afloat understands how to behave in the event of a capsize.

In a tragic incident in a south coast harbour, a nine-year-old child drowned when a powered dory capsized close to a pontoon during a journey which had been undertaken as a Plan B after a planned dinghy sailing session was cancelled due to adverse weather. The child was trapped under the capsized hull. No head count had been made after the rest of the party were recovered by a fishing boat in the vicinity, and the child's absence was not immediately realised.

Often, one of the more prosaic difficulties to be managed in sailing sessions is the launching and recovery of craft. This typically involves manhandling of heavy or waterlogged boats on the treacherous surface of the well named slipway. Advice on safe lifting is desirable, together with good footwear.

Man overboard drill is important, especially so for sailors operating without an instructor on board. A person floating separate from the boat can be hard to spot both by the rest of the crew and by those aboard any rescue craft.

Some sailing schools issue dinghy sailors with protective helmets to guard against a sudden impact with the vessel's boom, typically when an unplanned gybe occurs. This precaution is not universally adopted and the rate of injury from this cause seems to be small.

Yachting

'Sail training' uses yachts or large sailing vessels as a medium for adventure education. Seafarers have a culture strong in prudence and safety but also one that places great emphasis on self-reliance. This leads to some awkward decision-making when there is a potential conflict between traditional approaches and a modern concept of duty of care. Skippers may be qualified as master mariners but this does not automatically bring expertise in the management of anxious young adults in a potentially hazardous situation.

Skippers need to be sure that the prevailing arrangements are appropriate to the abilities of the crew, who may have little or no previous experience. A regime requiring trainees to be attached by lifelines when out of the cockpit, or at all times in bad weather or after dark, is worth consideration. Many experienced sailors will not wear a PFD in moderate conditions, but, since the instinct for self-protection is likely to be less well developed in novices, permanent wearing of buoyancy may be desirable for them.

Deckhands on ships of the line would be expected to work high aloft reefing and setting sails without any protection other than their own tenacity of grip. Working in such an environment is a fantastic experience for a young person but most parents would expect that there would be some additional security arrangements such as strategically placed nets or lifelines. Whenever an arrangement like a lifeline is used it is wise to consider what happens after the slip. If a person ends up suspended some way below a yard their subsequent retrieval may be far from simple.

Adverse conditions bring such a dramatic transformation that it can be very hard for the lay person to appreciate the difficulties and dangers that may ensue. The Marine Accident Investigation Branch (MAIB) publish salutary reports on accidents. They regularly identify poor stability or construction as contributory factors in serious marine accidents but human error is, of course, also prominent. It is important in any activity to have realistic training for instructors that helps them to engage with the real difficulties of what can sound to be a simple process.

A heavily built man of 40 lost his life when he fell overboard from a 22-foot keelboat after an inadvertent gybe. He was well equipped with a life jacket and sailing waterproofs over fleece clothing and was quickly reached by the rescue craft but, because of his size, could not be recovered into the boat. The water temperature was about 11 degrees Celsius. After about four minutes alongside the rescue craft the casualty lost consciousness and soon after stopped breathing.

Open canoes

Open canoeing, sometimes called Canadian canoeing, is a very popular activity in outdoor education and, as people realise the craft's potential for voyaging, the number of recreational users is growing fast. Open canoes are relatively stable and less intimidating to beginners than kayaks. Commonly, larger canoes will be operated with two paddlers in each boat.

Because beginners can rapidly acquire the basic paddling skills, satisfying journeys can readily be undertaken. However, it should always be kept in view that open water journeys on large inland lakes or on the sea are committing enterprises that are exceptionally vulnerable to sudden deteriorations in weather conditions. Fierce downdraughts from the mountains can produce a sudden all-in capsize – a worst case scenario for the leader. Such scenarios should be practised during training.

The other area of vulnerability for open boats is in rapids. Because the boat is un-decked it can rapidly swamp, so careful control and accurate judgement are necessary.

Although boats are usually constructed with some degree of reserve buoyancy, it is good practice to supplement this in order to guarantee that the craft is unsinkable and that, in the event of a capsize, it floats high enough in the water to ease emptying and righting.

A painter should be fitted and a substantial bailer or bucket carried in order to deal quickly with any swamping.

Although some providers use additional safety craft, BCU recommendations are that, in most conditions, the expertise present in the instructor and the group should be sufficient to deal with any emergency without external assistance. This admirable policy of self-reliance does depend upon well trained and well qualified instructors capable of making appropriate decisions in the field.

Starting a three-day open canoe expedition in South Africa

Sometimes canoes will be rafted together by being lashed to transverse spars. This improves stability considerably and so is often used for inexperienced paddlers operating with a headwind or with a degree of chop on the water. What must be avoided is using rafting to justify going out in what would otherwise be unacceptable conditions. Rafts can capsize or break up, in each case with potentially more serious consequences than a single canoe because of the risks of entrapment. In addition, rafts ride bigger waves less well than a properly handled single boat and so are more prone to swamping.

Rafted canoes may be effectively sailed downwind with an improvised rig. This is very popular with learners but care should be taken that they are not able to travel so fast as to be able to escape the immediate supervision of the instructor. The use of rafted canoes should be given a separate risk assessment and supervising staff should have practised their use in a variety of conditions. Towing rafts is problematical and should be done at low speed and by staff familiar with the process.

A serious near miss incident which culminated in rafted canoes being put under tow in choppy seas and increasing wind led the MAIB to emphasise the value of scenario-based training for hybrid activities of this kind. The situation is thought to have been made worse because of a blurring of the decision-making process by the different expectations of instructors and client and by confusion over whether this activity was to be treated as rafting or canoeing.

Kayak

Kayaking is another paddling discipline widely used in outdoor education. Craft are generally used individually, are much more manoeuvrable than open canoes and because they are decked, and often used with a spray deck as a barrier to water entering, can be used more readily on white water. Instructor skills in the two disciplines of kayaking and open canoeing are not readily transferable one to the other since there are distinct differences in group management, rescue techniques and so on.

On flat water the hazards are primarily environmental – cold water and adverse weather – but there is also a possibility of entrapment in the cockpit after capsize. Modern design has done much to eliminate this hazard but beginners can be intimidated. Two medical hazards to which paddlers are exposed are the occurrence of leptospirosis, a waterborne disease transmitted via the urine of rats, and 'surfer's ear', a progressive deafness arising from persistent exposure to cold water.

Moving water hazards are much more specific and can be at a high level in more challenging water. A characteristic of these hazards is that most emergencies will develop with great suddenness and must be resolved without loss of time – the victim may be held underwater. Many hazards are variations on a theme of entrapment by the combination of an obstacle and the force of the current:

- low overhanging branches can capsize and trap a boat;
- the boat and/or paddler can be carried by the force of the current into a 'strainer' – a narrowing through which the water passes but the boat or swimmer does not.

In some conditions the re-circulation of water directly below the entry point of a fall of water may also cause a counter-flow or tow-back that can hold a boat or a swimmer. Such a pattern of flow is usually called a stopper. In certain conformations of rock or in the geometric confines of a weir they can trap a person or hold them underwater for long periods.

Advanced paddlers will be aware of many other variations. The simple lesson is that moving-water kayak and canoe sessions need to be staffed by skilled and experienced instructors who are familiar with these hazards and how to deal with them. In the right hands and with careful choice of water, paddle sports have an excellent safety record.

Sea paddling

Introductory sessions in canoes and kayaks can be operated perfectly well in sheltered locations, but more extended sea journeys should be recognised as serious undertakings and staffed, equipped and organised accordingly. A sudden deterioration in water or sea state can cause great difficulties and adverse tidal streams or adverse wind can be very tiring to paddlers. These were important factors in the Lyme Bay disaster in 1993.

Surfing in kayaks or with special 'surf shoes' is an exciting activity. Great care must be taken to avoid offshore winds and offshore tide rips, which could carry a paddler or a swimmer out to sea. Good discipline is necessary and swimmers and surfers should be segregated to avoid dangerous collisions. A watcher on the beach is desirable.

Swimming

Swimming has always seemed to me to be a bit of a paradox. It is one of the few activities in an adventure programme that most people will have had a chance to do previously. It is a difficult activity to manage. The instructor has to tread a difficult line between the ludicrous and the terrifying. 'Yes, I know you regularly swim off the beach in Mallorca but here I want you to stay within chest height' sounds vaguely ridiculous but providers have also got to address the fact that lots of people drown in recreational settings (very few in organised activities) and that stronger swimmers are often the victims.

The answer has to be in a thoughtful process of risk assessment. Some of the controls to be considered might include:

- having a clearly defined area, perhaps marked with buoys, to limit swimming, where depth is less than chest height on the smallest swimmer;

- having a swimming test and applying restrictions on area or the providing of special equipment to poor swimmers;

- having all swimming supervised by a trained life saver who is on lookout, not in the water;

- having swimming take place in small numbers so that head count can be readily assessed;

- having a clear and recognised recall signal.

Swimming in uncontrolled areas like mountain tarns presents many hazards – cold water, poor visibility, unknown underfoot conditions, steep shelving banks and so on. Experience has shown that restricting people to, say, 'chest height' can go badly wrong in cold water and on uneven surfaces.

Land activities

Walking

Country walking is a generally benign activity but fields stocked with animals should be treated with caution. Coastal walks may have sections of path close to cliff edges and if ongoing erosion is occurring care is needed.

Much the greatest hazard lies with traffic. A group of walkers in a narrow country lane are extremely vulnerable should a vehicle travelling at high speed appear. The best advice is, wherever possible, to avoid road walking, especially in large groups. When there is no reasonable alternative, responsible individuals at front and back should keep a disciplined line and give clear warnings when any approaching vehicle is heard. Fluorescent waistcoats for back markers can help.

Adult parties are especially vulnerable when travelling to and from the pub at night. Reflective clothing and torches help – a taxi is probably best.

Hill walking is a less spectacular activity than climbing overhanging rock or ice but it can present at least as many hazards. Any problems tend to be exacerbated by the remoteness of the activity from immediate assistance and the increased severity of mountain weather. Wind speed and precipitation increase about threefold when one goes from sea level to 1,000 metres. In many areas, the topography makes the use of mobile phones uncertain and planning should reflect this.

Minor slips and twisted ankles are common. The most serious hazards are major falls, exhaustion hypothermia, drowning in swollen rivers or mountain lakes, lightning strikes and rock falls. In hot conditions, heatstroke and dehydration should be added to the list.

The risk of major falls in summer conditions can be expected to be confined to rugged terrain and their occurrence is usually a result of serious errors of route finding, often combined with a serious loss of group control.

When young people travel on multi-day journeys unaccompanied by adult leaders their opportunity for satisfying achievement is enhanced, but so may their vulnerability when things go wrong. Such ventures will usually be the culmination of extended training and practice; provision of that training together with proper checks and well thought-out procedures in the event of an emergency are the best guarantee of security (see Chapter 8).

Water hazards in the mountains are of great importance. The innocuous trickle that you skipped across this morning can be fed by the freshets from sudden mountain storms to become a fierce torrent within a few hours. A number of tragedies have arisen from an underestimation of the dangers presented by such streams and by an unwillingness to accept the delay of diversion to a safer route. Except as a last resort in a pressing emergency, crossing a dangerous spate river is best avoided, even by those trained to do it.

In the mountains, hypothermia, the reduction of core body temperature to dangerous levels, usually affects people who are already exhausted and demoralised. Modern protective clothing and equipment is effective in most weather conditions; the weak link is often how the person uses it. Characteristically, on a wet and windy day, the hill walker who is heading towards hypothermia is apathetic or unusually belligerent, lags at the back of the party and cannot be bothered to zip up a jacket, put on a hat or eat some food. This is not bloody mindedness but the early signs of a serious condition that every competent leader should recognise. If not dealt with promptly (such as by stopping or modifying the route, arranging food, hot drinks and additional clothing) a life-threatening situation can rapidly develop.

I once had overall responsibility for a number of 18 year olds who, in small groups, were completing unaccompanied three-day expeditions through the Lakeland hills in unusually hot weather. At about nine in the evening my phone rang. A group member had run to the public phone to tell me that one of his companions had been taken ill, was shivering violently, complaining of the cold and becoming delirious. Not unreasonably, the casualty's companions had put the shivering person into a warm sleeping bag inside the tent. It rapidly struck me that the ambient temperature was still above 30°C and that we were probably dealing with heatstroke, which occurs when overheating of the body core affects brain function and which can result in coma and death. Such a condition requires urgent cooling. Picking up a doctor on the way, we raced to the group's campsite and a found a young man who was barely conscious, incoherent and quite obviously seriously ill.

The doctor's rapid diagnosis confirmed my suspicions, but his treatment was unexpected. The casualty was briskly taken out of the sleeping bag and gallon after gallon of cold water from the river was poured over him. Within a few minutes the lad was almost back to normal – an astonishingly rapid recovery as the drastic treatment brought his core temperature back to normal levels.

We had been fortunate to avoid a disaster largely because of the preparation that had taken place:

- the group were trained to deal with emergencies;
- they had an emergency contact number which was manned;
- the call triggered an appropriate level of response.

However, we felt that although the group had the generic skills to deal with this emergency, our training tended to be focused on the much more common hazard of cold weather. We learnt that with expected hot weather, training should include an awareness of heatstroke and dehydration and how to address both conditions.

The dark waters of mountain tarns are tempting on a hot day but the leader needs to control the activity carefully; unexpectedly cold water a short way beneath the surface and a shelving or irregular bed make swimming a far from innocuous activity. Limiting the depth of entry to chest height reduces but certainly does not eliminate the hazard.

Mountains are used as a metaphor for permanence, yet the reality is different. Progressive weathering loosens and releases rocks which can be enormous, but accidents result when one person unintentionally knocks a rock onto another. Careful spacing and routeing of the group can control this and it is also prudent to avoid travelling up narrow gullies or steep boulder fields behind another party.

Camping

Wild camping is a great adventure for young people and one that allows extended journeys and a unique quality of interaction with the natural world.

Undoubtedly the biggest threats arise from cooking and the use of stoves, either from scalds or burns. There is much to be said for using cold rations for a simple overnight camp for beginners but, equally, camp cooking can be a new and unfamiliar skill of great educational value. However, time and attention must be given to proper training and supervision.

Cooking inside a small tent or in the tent porch should be outlawed for all but the most experienced and competent. When I was a student I saw a neighbouring tent destroyed in a few seconds when a flapping door caught light on the stove. Fortunately, the occupant and one-time cook was able to dive out of the rear entry to the tent and was unharmed.

Two types of stove are in common use; those using pressurised gas cylinders and those of the Trangia type using alcohol burning in a small metal cup. Gas stoves are convenient, and if equipped with a self-sealing valve are generally safe in use. But a trace of grit can spoil the seal with the burner, causing a gas leak and many gas stoves are spindly unstable affairs that make a tipped pot of boiling water a particular threat. They are often ineffective in windy conditions so there can be a strong temptation to take them inside the tent.

Alcohol stoves are wonderfully simple with no real moving parts, and are usually a stable, integrated structure of burner, pans and windshield. They often burn very effectively in wind, albeit with reduced fuel economy. The problems are mainly concerned with refuelling, which is done by pouring liquid fuel into the burner. Alcohol flames can be difficult to discern in bright light and so it is common for people to inadvertently pour fuel onto a naked flame. Even the hot metal of a recently extinguished burner can be sufficient to ignite the fuel.

A tragic event unrolled a few years ago when, on the last evening of an extended journey, a group were camping on a warm evening in a valley campsite. One boy was cooking, another lying on the ground next to him, wearing only shorts and T-shirt. As the cook attempted to refuel the stove the fuel caught light, flared back into the bottle which erupted a column of flame. The cook shied back and dropped the now burning bottle which spewed burning fuel over the second boy, who ran in panic, further fanning the flames and suffering extensive burns.

Careful training and supervision by the leader are crucial. Some instructors insist that younger groups get them to refuel the stove, others that several minutes elapse before an extinguished burner is refilled. Some fuel bottles have an emergency cut-out that restricts spillage in the event of a flare-up. Having an exclusion zone around the cooker for all except the cook improves the safety of bystanders and also reduces the hazard of spillage of hot liquids. A recently developed jelly fuel for alcohol stoves promises to reduce some of these hazards.

Finally, it should be mentioned that after a hard day, although the instructor may be sorely tempted to adjourn to his tent, the need for a degree of supervision continues.

Rock climbing

Single-pitch rock climbing should be one of the safest activities used in outdoor education, high on apparent and very low on actual risk. There seem to be more injuries to participants walking to and from the climbing site than ever occur during the activity.

Single pitch climbing, belayed from the foot of the cliff

Hazards to be considered include rock fall, anchor failure, misuse of equipment and failures of belaying, slips and pendulum swings but the biggest area of concern does not affect participants. Before a suitably protected top-rope climbing session takes place a responsible person has to rig the crag, placing anchors and arranging the ropes. Staff doing this are in a potentially hazardous position and may find it difficult to give complete attention to their own safety. It is highly advisable that whenever the people rigging the crag are in a position where a slip could have serious consequences, they must be attached to an anchor, this usually being done with a rigging rope and a moveable attachment such as a prussik loop or a rope clamp.

Anchors are usually used redundantly with so much duplication that anchor failure should be a remote possibility, but failure of belaying (the securing of the climber's rope to hold any slip) is a much more likely threat when that belaying is done by an inexperienced person.

A responsible person needs to supervise closely a novice belayer, and, initially at least, should be in sufficiently close proximity to be able to physically intervene by taking the control rope. Thus the spacing of belayers is the primary factor in determining what ratio of supervision is necessary. Except in favourable situations it is desirable for one instructor to have no more than two novice belayers to supervise.

The rock fall hazard is greatest on crags that only get occasional use, where loose rock may lie undisturbed. It is desirable for staff to have carefully swept the crag, removing loose material in advance of the site being used for groups. The likely scenario is that a climber dislodges a rock or drops a piece of equipment which then hits someone beneath. Paradoxically, people on the ground are usually much more at risk from rock fall than those on the rope and so, wherever possible, spectators should be outside the 'impact zone' and everyone should wear helmets. A classic error of the inexperienced is to only equip the person climbing with a helmet. Fatal accidents to spectators have occurred in this way.

Although not a life-threatening problem, an extremely common cause of ankle injury is sloppy belaying in the first few feet of a climb. I encourage novice belayers to keep the rope as tight as possible until the climber is a couple of metres up so that, in the event of a slip, the climber will not hit the ground on the rope stretch. Once higher than this, security is greatly improved.

The security of the belayed climber is at its greatest when they are vertically beneath the anchor; when they depart from this line a fall is likely to result in a pendulum. Except when short, this can result in bumps and scrapes or more serious injury. Crags where the natural conformation of the rock tends to the diagonal are more difficult in this respect because not only is this the line that the climb may be forced to follow, instructors can have their perception of the vertical distorted.

Equipment errors, such as incorrectly fastened harness buckles or incorrectly threaded belay devices, are much more likely to occur when the instructor is under time pressure or another distraction. It is desirable for climbing to be staffed by a minimum of two instructors, in order to improve the quality of supervision and to allow one to focus on group management while the other undertakes rigging or installation.

Climbing walls

Artificial climbing walls are very popular as an activity in their own right as well as being very good training aids for climbers. Many of the uncertainties of 'real' climbing have been eliminated but walls are not risk free! Most accidents that occur are as a result of belayer error or the incorrect fitting or attachment of harnesses. Several cases have occurred where climbers have inadvertently clipped the protection rope into the flimsy plastic gear loops on the harness instead of the main strong point. When a slip occurs, the fragile loop breaks and a serious fall results.

Abseiling

Abseiling, also known as rappelling, is usually offered as part of a climbing session and shares many of the same issues such as the difficulty of diagonal lines. The worst case would be catastrophic anchor failure and it is normal to guard against this by the separation of two different anchor systems, one for the abseil rope (which is slid down) and another, the safety rope, to protect the novice.

It is good practice to use what is called a releasable abseil to guard against the possibility of the descending person being unable to continue as a result of a rope tangle or of hair or clothing jammed in the abseil device. In that event, the rope is released and the abseiler lowered to the ground on the safety rope.

Multi-pitch climbing

The great advantage of single-pitch climbing is that, should difficulties ensue, the climber is normally within easy lowering distance of the ground. Multi-pitch climbs are of greater length (usually longer than a single rope length) and what can be a minor problem on a single-pitch crag can present the greatest difficulties when the party is a hundred metres or more from the ground. Because of this a higher-level instructional qualification is required and smaller operational ratios are used.

This increased cost means that few adventure providers are able to offer the unique experience of multi-pitch climbing. Few accidents occur.

Winter mountaineering

Those instructing mountain activities usually separate summer and winter conditions. In winter conditions, snow and ice transform the mountains and the skills of winter mountaineering, particularly the use of ice axe and crampons, are necessary for safe travel. In its broad sense, winter mountaineering can be considered to include hill walking such as an ascent in winter conditions of Snowdon, mountaineering such as a traverse of the Aonach Eagach Ridge in Glencoe, and snow and ice climbing on graded climbs such as the Central Gully on Great End.

The presence or absence of winter conditions is an important factor to be considered during the winter months. This presence or absence has a considerable effect on the difficulties likely to be encountered, the hazards likely to be faced, the necessary equipment to be carried or deployed and, not least, on the level of skill and qualification of the leader.

'Summer conditions' is a term that covers everything else, when either snow and ice is absent from the planned route or the snow present is of a limited extent and not likely to demand special winter techniques. Summer conditions can be found high on British mountains on any day of the year but are much less likely to occur during the winter months.

Correspondingly, winter conditions can also occur throughout the year but would generally be confined to within the period November to April inclusive or a little longer on northern hills.

Some authorities identify a further category of intermediate conditions when snow and ice is present but is easily avoided or does not demand the skills of the winter mountaineer. An example of the latter would be the case when a single snowfall has left a sprinkling of soft powdery snow on bare hillsides. Often, in such conditions, a hill walker could be expected to be able to get a secure footing without the need for ice axe or crampons.

If snow is present it requires a high level of experience to determine whether winter or intermediate conditions apply. When snow lies, it is a decision of some gravity to allow instructors only qualified for 'summer' conditions to operate on the basis of a judgement that intermediate conditions apply and the full skills of a winter mountaineer are not required. This is usually a decision to be made by a well qualified 'technical adviser'.

Similar primary hazards apply to all of the winter mountaineering activities, being slips and falls, severe weather and avalanche.

Falls regularly occur in conditions of hard frozen snow. Such conditions demand a good level of skill in axe and crampon work and are extremely unforgiving in the event of error. Casualties will often have fallen several hundred feet before smashing into boulder fields.

The severity of winter weather can defy belief, with intense precipitation and winds often well in excess of one hundred miles per hour. The cooling effect on participants is obvious, but severe weather is also very disorientating, and frequently contributes to errors of judgement, navigation or avalanche avoidance.

Whenever snow lies on mountains avalanches are a possibility. They are a familiar peril in skiing areas such as the Alps but are also an important threat to winter mountaineers on British hills. Under the wrong conditions, any snow covered slope steeper than about 25 degrees can avalanche

These comments will suffice to make the point that winter mountaineering is a demanding activity requiring high standards of leadership, fitness and commitment from participants, who are themselves willing to engage with the significant residual risk of the sport. Winter mountaineering is not an activity where risk is merely perceived.

Except in the most accessible and controlled environments, I do not consider winter mountaineering an activity for children on general adventure programmes. Minors cannot normally be asked to make the distinctly adult decisions about the intrinsic risks involved in winter mountaineering. However, we cannot ignore the fact that some teenagers have a passionate interest in the hills and it can certainly be argued that it is better for them to develop their passion and skills under the wise guidance of a more experienced person.

In such cases, it can be important for a continuing dialogue about risk, challenge and safety to include the young person, the instructor and parents or guardians. Progression in the sport should normally be cautious and measured.

One of the shattering tragedies of outdoor education in Britain took place in November 1971 in the area of the Feith Buidhe, a stream traversing a wide, shallow depression high on the Cairngorm plateau when six school children perished in the snow.

The city of Edinburgh had given great importance to outdoor education in its schools and the success of this work in inspiring pupils was the envy of many. Ainsley Park School had, like other Edinburgh schools, an outdoor specialist on its permanent staff. This teacher, Ben Beattie was an experienced mountaineer and, under his enthusiastic influence, many children had not only sampled outdoor activities but had gone on to actively engage as participants well beyond the novice level.

On the fateful November day, two groups of pupils, mostly 15 year olds, set off separately from the chairlift on Cairn Gorm; seven, who were judged as particularly strong, with Beattie, and six plus one other person with Cathy Davidson, who although a capable mountaineer was somewhat less experienced than Beattie. In deteriorating weather, Beattie shortened his planned and ambitious route and, instead, spent the night in the Curran Bothy, a bare aluminium dog-kennel, near to Lochan Buidhe and often covered in snow except for an indicator post.

Unknown to him, Cathy Davidson's group were a few hundred metres away, invisible in the low cloud and the blowing snow, fighting the weather and desperately trying to find the shelter of the Curran Bothy before nightfall. They were unsuccessful and, with a badly tired party and still worsening conditions, Davidson had little choice but to prepare an emergency bivouac using the desperately limited shelter of plastic bags and scrapes in the shallow snow.

Next morning, Beattie's party found conditions even worse. He assumed, incorrectly and with momentous consequences, that Davidson, in light of the poor conditions, had returned to Cairn Gorm and the valley on the previous day and so, unaware of the unfolding tragedy, led his own party, with difficulty down the steep March Burn to the Lairig Ghru and eventually back to the road at Loch Morlich.

Beattie was met there by the recently appointed head of Lagganlia, an Edinburgh outdoor centre in the area, and only then was it realised that Davidson's party was not back at base but was almost certainly still on the mountain.

It was after nightfall on this, the second day, when the first advance parties of rescuers set out, in hopelessly difficult blizzard conditions, to search the enormous extent of the plateau. Cathy Davidson had struggled a little way towards help but all her party had now to face another forced bivouac.

The following morning, conditions eased a little and visibility improved. A helicopter carrying rescuers found Davidson, who with tremendous courage and perseverance was still fighting her way to get help for the party, *in extremis* on the slopes of Cairn Lochain and she was able to direct them to the rest of the party. When found, six were dead and only one boy had survived.

Cycling

Mountain biking is an exciting and increasingly popular adventure activity which can encompass a wide range of performance from simple journeys on wide and gentle forest trails through to multi-day expeditions or extremely steep and demanding descents on rough ground. A recent development has been the construction of purpose-built biking trails, often provided in a dedicated area with graded and mapped trails and support facilities.

The sport is subject to some misapprehensions. Because it is often believed that 'anyone can ride a bike' it is easy to be persuaded that the management of the activity is a simple business, easily accomplished by any reasonably sensible instructor. In fact, this type of biking is relatively hazardous, with considerable potential for accident, so it requires and deserves high-quality leadership and management.

Supplying the bike itself can be problematical. Many regular providers have found that it is attractive to subcontract the regular supply and maintenance of bikes to a specialist supplier. Failure of brakes or steering can be catastrophic on steep ground or in traffic so well prepared equipment and thorough pre-ride checks are vital. Wise instructors pay attention to sizing the bike to the participant and ensuring adequate personal and protective clothing, which should normally include, helmet, gloves, eye protection and non-baggy clothing (to avoid entangling with the chain and chainwheels). Some practice in a controlled area is desirable to ensure competent control before moving into more hazardous terrain and to identify the occasional person who has never ridden a bike.

Road biking sits more comfortably with conventional sports but mountain bikers will often access open country by riding along public roads. Far from being the simple approach to the real challenge of the day that it might appear, travel on busy roads can be highly dangerous for groups of cyclists, especially those not yet in confident control of their bikes. A responsible leader and back marker, bright clothing and prearranged methods of travel are desirable but much the best solution is to avoid busy roads and those prone to use by heavy freight vehicles.

I once went out to some forest trails with a group of bikers in their early teens but to get the forest the only realistic route gave us a worrying three-mile journey on a narrow but busy road with huge timber trucks thundering past every few minutes. It was a great relief for everyone to finally arrive in the forest. These groups still go to the same forest, but now bikes and riders travel by van and trailer to the forest edge – an awkward decision to have made in the context of a green activity like cycling, but undoubtedly a safer method of operation.

On steep ground the problem is largely about control of speed. Instructors can coach, train and advise but it is the rider him or herself who has to pull the brake lever at the right time. Some people freeze in panic, others entirely misjudge the speed while others, often young men, would rather be sorry than safe. All are inclined to end up in a heap at the bottom of a steep slope. The leader has to put great effort into maintaining good control of speed but it would be foolish to pretend that this is easy. Staying on flat ground is probably the most effective method but at the cost of a certain amount of excitement.

Any cycle trail that cuts across a hillside is a threat, because a loss of control may result in a big fall on the downhill side. A couple of close escapes occurred when cyclists came off their bikes on a trail that snaked across a bank above a fast-flowing river. The key consideration was for the instructor to realise that the issue was not just how difficult was the trail (not very), more importantly it was also about the consequences if someone did lose control and leave the track (which were severe). There is nothing wrong with getting learners with poor bike control skills to walk across such a section.

Shortly after being persuaded that it was no longer acceptable to treat biking as something any instructor could do, I took part in an excellent training course for mountain bike instructors. After a few days of excellent progress we headed for one of best mountain bike sites in Scotland and enjoyed some excellent, moderate trails.

Towards the end of the day (the first warning sign), we found ourselves adjacent to the downhill course, where one of the team, a cyclist who was familiar with the location, suggested that we could cross over to the downhill course. Since the downhill is normally frequented by bikers in body armour riding bikes with heavy duty suspension and brakes, concerns were expressed about the wisdom of this. These concerns fell from view (the second warning sign) when we were reassured by one of the locals, 'The course is very quiet midweek and, in any case, the downhillers make so much noise that we would have lots of time to get off the course before anyone arrived.'

The trainer did not take much part in this, the detour was not part of the main plan (the third warning sign) and he was in charge of a group of other professional instructors with the result that authority, expertise and judgement had become spread out so that it was somewhat unclear with whom they lay (the fourth warning sign). One might think that this plethora of warning signs would have led to such a collection of experts making a prudent decision. Far from it. We all launched on to the course, and, within minutes of starting, were so absorbed in the thrill of it all that any doubts were suppressed (the fifth warning sign). If anyone still had concerns they were never voiced (yes, the sixth warning sign).

We had just descended, amid many whoops and yells, a particularly steep section. Some of the team found this so thrilling that they were pushing bikes back up to have another go, the rest of us clustered in a small huddle at its foot. I do not know who heard the clatter and yell first but, faster than thought, and certainly before anyone could be warned, we all caught sight of a downhiller at the top of the steep slope, in full gear and in full flight, about three metres off the ground and travelling at fifty miles per hour or more, his mouth wide open and screaming. A second later, another rider followed.

Sometimes, you can do the most stupid things and get away totally unscathed. Despite the near perfect target of ten people and bikes on the main part of the track, neither of the high-speed riders, who had every right to be there, hit anyone or anything, and even more remarkable, were not themselves unseated. A different roll of the dice and we could have had several people in hospital – or worse.

We shamefacedly made our way down to the foot of the course where the two riders were taking off their helmets and gave our grovelling apologies. Downhillers are often accused of having the worst traits of the young male – lack of consideration and abrasiveness, if, not aggression. I can only say that these two were exceptionally measured in their response – we deserved a much more severe tongue lashing for nearly killing them, for being where we had no right to be and, above all, for having ignored so many clear signals.

Hybrid activities

Adventure activities have expanded beyond the mainstream activities such hill walking, canoeing and sailing to include 'hybrid' activities such as gorge scrambling, plunge pools, 'coasteering' and raft building.

These activities tend to emphasise the element of fun and may make lesser demands of fitness or physical aptitude on participants than more traditional activities. Also, the requirements of specialist equipment can often be much reduced. These factors can make such hybrid activities particularly suitable for and popular with school groups.

Various activities such as ghyll or gorge scrambling involve travelling on foot along watercourses. On occasions, these journeys include exciting free jumps into deep plunge pools. Sometimes, the site for these jumps is readily accessible and then the plunge pool can be undertaken as a challenging activity in its own right.

However, these newer, less formal adventure activities present significant differences from those that are more established. Firstly, they do not generally have an established national governing body scheme of training or instructor qualification. Secondly, the activities do not usually have any recognised grading scheme for difficulties such as exists for, say, rock climbing or white-water kayaking. These differences can cause difficulties in both risk assessment and in the selection of supervisory staff.

By illustration, the appropriate qualification for gorge scrambling would commonly be seen as the Mountain Instructor Award. Holders would be very good at assessing and managing groups in the rocky terrain of gorges but might have a relatively slight knowledge of water hazards. They may be a very good choice to lead in a 'dryish' gorge, but less so in one with many waterfalls or plunge pools. Conversely, qualified paddlers would be very strong on moving water hazards but may have less depth of understanding on the rocky sections. It could be argued that cavers would be particularly well qualified because underground they regularly deal with slippery rock, flowing water and so on. What is required is a qualified and responsible person to decide what mix of qualification and experience is appropriate for a particular activity at a particular site.

Hybrid activities can be exposed to significant levels of risk, which, as a result of the lack of specific training, can escape recognition. Each activity needs a specific process of risk assessment, specific training and specific authorisation of staff.

Gorge scrambling

Water temperature and water depth or speed of flow should be taken into account in the daily risk assessment. 'Go' and 'no go' levels might be defined. Hazards include:

- obstacles such as tree branches or debris such as barbed wire perhaps carried in by flood water;

- a person getting a foot trapped by an underwater obstacle and held under by the force of flow;

- insufficient depth in 'plunge pools' so that jumpers hit the bottom;

- rock fall from side walls.

Improvised raft building

This usually employs plastic drums, wooden spars and lashing ropes. The normal hazards of any water activity are present with in addition:

Rafting. In a sheltered bay and in calm weather an open canoe gives adequate safety cover. The instructor is wearing a dry suit and buoyancy aid and is carrying a knife and a throw line. A second instructor is on shore.

- a danger of entrapment in the event of capsize or disintegration of the raft;
- a risk of injury by scissoring of poorly lashed spars;

- possible contamination from the previous contents of barrels;

- unsafe lifting during construction or launching.

Close supervision is necessary. Instructors should carry a rope-cutting tool and be equipped to enter the water if necessary. Some kind of safety craft is normally used.

Structures

Ropes courses, trapeze jumps, zip wires, Jacob's ladders, and other variants on the theme are exciting activities in wide use. They usually involve some sort of challenging activity at height and are normally constructed rather than being of natural formation. There are now a number of specialist companies who specialise in the design, build and maintenance of these structures.

The two hazards to be considered in the management of the activity are falls and possible strangulation. There is no standard approach and many different means of protection have evolved, usually based on one of:

- belaying with a rope;

- protection with cow's tails – two portable anchor lines that are clipped into a protection cable;

- continuous rail protection;

- protection by nets or other means of confinement.

Human error in clipping or belaying is a significant concern and efforts should be made to minimise this risk. Low-level elements where participants can practise clipping, an effective buddy system, good staffing ratios and clear sight lines are all to be considered. Continuous rail systems greatly reduce this risk.

If a person slips on a high-level element they may end up suspended from their protection link. Instructors must have practised rescue techniques and have the necessary equipment available. Rescue from cow's tail systems can be technically challenging. This would make a background in climbing desirable in instructors.

Group games

Various problem-solving and challenge activities are in use, often as a medium for team development. They have a light-hearted feel but consideration of the risks should remain in view. Slips are commonplace so a good landing is desirable. Helmets are often worn.

'Spotting' is often used in some form. Other group members guard the person on the element, standing in close proximity and ready to intervene in the event of a slip, by steadying or catching the faller. Spotting is often done very poorly and then makes only an illusory contribution to safety. To be effective it must be confined to low-level elements, and spotters must be physically capable of the task and must be well trained and practised.

Underground activities

Caves and mines take you into a completely different world. Even the simplest excursion is a tremendous experience for youngsters, total silence, total darkness and surroundings like a sci-fi film set. However, the cave environment can also be an intimidating one to an inexperienced person – claustrophobic, cold, wet, dark, the sound of rushing water, apparently bottomless drops – so that a very simple terrain by the standards of the experienced caver can produce high levels of anxiety in a novice, particularly in an unfit or poorly motivated novice.

Mines, originally developed for the extraction of copper, slate, plumbago, gypsum and other minerals, have been used for adventure activities. They can be tremendously impressive places with the additional interest of living industrial archaeology, but they often present an uncertain and difficult to control environment. Roof falls are not uncommon in some mines and others may have treacherous timber floors. Unusually stringent risk assessments would be the norm before deciding to use a mine for exploration with children – but this can be done successfully in the right place.

The hazard of prime concern in caving is flooding. In the wrong conditions any stream cave or pothole can flood, so careful monitoring of river levels and weather forecasts is essential. Some systems or passages will have a reputation for being safe from flood water or will have a refuge section that stays dry, but, of course, there is always a first time for anything. Construction works on the surface, even distant ones, can affect drainage through the system and passages can be excavated as part of cave exploration with the same effect. Once in a century cloudbursts do occur.

Simple walk-in caves are generally rapid of access and egress, but more technical caves with squeezes or pitches can be very time-consuming and extremely tiring for beginners. Skilled cavers can get through remarkably narrow squeezes but a cautious approach is desirable for novices.

We now enjoy effective telephone or radio communication in many areas. Caves are an exception, so it is common to have a system of phone contact at the point of entry to and exit from the cave. In the event of illness or injury, evacuation from any but the most simple cave can be extremely difficult.

Some cave systems can have an accumulation of naturally occurring radioactive radon gas. This is primarily a hazard for people such as instructors who have repeated exposure.

New activities

New activities should be piloted carefully and then subjected to a thorough risk assessment before being used with real students. Decisions should be made about:

- whether the risk controls are at a sufficient level;
- what will be the operating procedures;
- what is a suitable operating ratio;
- how staff are to be trained and authorised.

In the early stages of implementation it is desirable to consider a higher staffing ratio and to have your most experienced staff in charge. The success or otherwise of the activity should be reviewed at regular intervals and, where necessary, changes made. When you have regularly run an activity for several years, you will have formed a fairly complete picture of the relevant safety issues, but the unexpected can still catch you out.

Chapter summary

- The most commonly offered activities are trekking, paddle sports and climbing.
- Also popular are sailing, gorge scrambling, rafting and mountain biking.
- Completely reliable fitting and use of critical safety equipment is vital.
- For water activities the risks of drowning, immersion cooling and adverse weather are prominent but hazards can be well controlled in most situations.
- For land activities, falls and slips and impact with falling objects are the primary hazards but other serious hazards arising from excessive cooling or overheating and adverse weather can occur.
- Hybrid activities present particular difficulties of management.
- New activities should be subjected to a proper process of screening and risk assessment to define their main safety issues.

Chapter 11

Emergency planning and response

Although we might make every effort to avoid things going wrong, anyone who engages regularly with adventure activities is likely to encounter some form of emergency situation, either occurring in their own group or as a result of an encounter with another party in difficulty. For organisations operating for many days each year, this likelihood rises to a near certainty. Furthermore, some parts of the operation will have important variables which are beyond our control; so, over a long period, one can expect that an emergency will, sooner or later, occur.

If sailing offshore for long enough, even the most prudent skipper will eventually encounter a severe gale. This can be usefully characterised as an 'expected' emergency – we do not know when or if the gale will occur but it is clear that our planning and preparation should include its possible occurrence. Anything that has been identified in our processes of risk assessment as an important hazard could, in the wrong circumstances, produce an emergency and the most likely of these will be 'expected'.

Similarly, a teacher regularly leading groups of 10 year olds on countryside walks for long enough is likely to encounter some kind of sudden illness affecting a child.

In contrast, unexpected emergencies emerge, as it were, from a blue sky, and are so outside our experience or forecasting capabilities as to be genuinely unpredictable.

Preparation and planning

There are both organisational and individual levels of preparation and planning.

Individual

To find oneself in a position of responsibility as an emergency flashes into existence is a frightening experience. It becomes all too clear that the right decisions and actions can save lives; the wrong choices can have devastating and far-reaching effects. This pressure adversely affects even the most experienced and best trained and can be entirely incapacitating for the ill-prepared.

Someone must take charge. Emergencies will rarely respond to a democratic approach so a leader is necessary and any leader is likely to be better than none, even a person uncertain of their capabilities under pressure. Once in charge, the leader should try to focus on the resolution of the emergency in an utterly concentrated manner and fight against distraction and mental clutter. For now, the consequences of the event, the effect on people's lives, the injustice of it all must be ignored and every effort put into addressing the emergency with calm efficiency.

A real emergency like an avalanche accident calls for prompt action and decisive leadership.

Hands-on involvement can be an almost irresistible temptation for the leader but whenever other assistance is at hand, the leader should aim to avoid this trap by delegating and directing others to do the essential tasks of first aid, making shelter, telephoning for help and so on. The leader's primary task is to resolve the local situation by making good decisions and avoiding bad ones. No emergency response will be perfect and every leader in a complex situation will make mistakes or at least not always make the best choices. When mistakes are made, time should not be wasted in self-recrimination but instead the leader should move on to try another approach.

People who have been put in such a situation have often found that they have risen to the challenge much more effectively than they would have previously expected. This is a reassurance together with the fact that the correct action in an emergency can often be simple – simple but rarely easy.

Field management

Emergency preparedness is yet another argument for having individuals of extensive activity and leadership experience in charge of adventure activities. This can be supported in a number of ways. Scenario-based training can have great value by simulating the pressure of decision-making that falls on the leader. I have been regularly involved in training leaders in various forms of mountain rescue, including avalanche recovery, that have made extensive use of scenarios. It is a privilege to be an observer of such simulations of emergency management.

During such practices, I have seen rescuers come to blows, leave a (simulated) casualty in the snow after losing count of the number of casualties recovered, drop the casualty, forget vital equipment, go to the wrong location and so on. Before dismissing this as rank incompetence it is worth remembering that the trainees were all individuals of a high level of skill and proven judgement, yet even they were not immune to the serious distractions of an emergency situation. The groups that were most effective in dealing with simulated emergencies already had a leader or quickly appointed one who:

- stayed outside the immediate action;
- took time to make a simple plan that was communicated to everyone;
- delegated tasks to others;
- was kept informed about progress;
- communicated instructions clearly;
- stayed calm;
- assessed developments and setbacks and, when necessary, re-planned.

In contrast, groups that were least effective in dealing with the simulations had no leader or one who tended to have:

- tried unsuccessfully to do everything him or herself;
- launched into immediate action;
- made no plan;
- shouted a great deal;
- failed to monitor progress;
- showed signs of panic;
- failed to re-plan in the light of new information or circumstances.

Virtually without exception, failures of management are the root cause of problems and delays in emergency response and training should highlight this.

Organisational

Bigger organisations are more likely to be able to deploy staff who can be dedicated to a particular emergency, but they are also more likely to need some recognised structure and protocol in dealing with emergencies and crises.

No two emergency situations are identical. Some are utterly outside of previous experience, so there is a limit to how specific emergency preparation can become without beginning to threaten a generic preparedness capable of producing an appropriate response to the completely unexpected occurrence. To deal with such unexpected emergencies we must fall back on general principles and rely on the standard systems of operation.

Even when there is a large element of the expected in the emergency the first steps to be taken are often the same. Typically these are:

- somebody takes charge;
- initial response to stabilise situation;
- inform a person or persons in authority;
- follow emergency plan.

The emergency plan is the previously agreed protocol for operating in an emergency and might include:

- a flow chart indicating priority actions for emergencies;
- contact details for key personnel, rescue services, medical assistance;
- guidelines for the most common expected emergencies.

Expected emergencies

If you have been operating for some time a combination of your records of previous incidents combined with your own experience and a generous dose of worst-case analysis will give an indication of the situations most likely to produce an emergency. Here are some to consider as a starting point for your own preparations:

Fire	Party lost or overdue
Vehicle accidents	Drowning
Medical emergencies	Heat or cold injury
Assaults and self-harm	Fast water
Falls from height	Severe weather
Falling objects	

Fire and vehicle accidents are at the top of this list because each has the high potential to result in multiple fatalities.

Having identified some of the main categories of 'expected' emergency it is useful to give some consideration to:

- what particular actions might be appropriate;
- what specific information might be important;
- what specific equipment might be important.

I heard a terrifying account, possibly apocryphal, of an oil company which had put a great deal of time and energy into training staff in emergency response scenarios. Every conceivable emergency situation had been identified and analysed; each would trigger an agreed response, and each was supported by training, checklists and defined procedures. No doubt these had proved effective on a number of occasions until, one day, a fire of unimaginable severity broke out.

Staff tried in vain to follow the standard procedures but the truth was these did not apply with much relevance to an incident of such scale. The scale of the event was beyond the imagination of the planners.

No procedure had instructed the responsible personnel to turn off the flow of oil to the burning installation because nobody had ever imagined that the entire structure could burn. For a long time oil continued to be pumped into the flames ... until somebody realised that this was outside of previous imagination, began to think for himself and turned off the oil.

Emergency file

It is of value to have some of the routine requirements of an emergency response organised in advance. A small organisation might have a dedicated grab file, a large one a dedicated office. Some of the things to be considered for inclusion are:

- ring bound book for use as incident log;
- pencils/pens;
- flip chart and/or whiteboard;
- dedicated telephone;
- maps of operating areas;
- contact details for rescue agencies, medical aid, emergency maintenance/services, vehicle hire.

Reputation

Should a serious emergency occur, there will often be the potential for an important impact upon the organisation's reputation and standing. It is important to recognise this in the way that information is released and managed, but above all, we should get our priorities right – the safety of those out in the field and the ethical treatment of parents or next of kin should be our prime concern.

Advance consideration of communication issues such as the issue of press releases, the control of telephones, the briefing of staff can help to keep the priorities in proper order without neglecting these other important areas.

Crisis management

For larger organisations, it can be useful to distinguish between an emergency and a crisis.

An *emergency* must be treated with careful and focused attention but can probably be resolved at a local level. It is likely that normal operation will be able to continue to some degree without limiting the resources available to the resolution of the emergency.

Emergencies may occur fairly frequently, perhaps every year or two.

A *crisis* is of such a magnitude that it may not be possible to resolve it with purely local assistance, it may need the dedicated attention of many or all staff and may prevent or seriously affect normal operation. Such situations are infrequent, but large-scale operators can expect to meet them from time to time. When they do occur the controller and the immediate support team must be able to devote total attention to the crisis.

A crisis plan can usefully identify who might be the members of such a crisis team, what circumstances would lead to the team being convened and how members are to be contacted in such an event. There may need to be specification of how an emergency is judged to have evolved into a crisis.

The controller

Being in charge of the overall response to an emergency or a crisis is an unenviable position. Many of the lessons of successful field management (listed above) apply, only even more so. It is essential to take the broad view and to delegate to others to engage with the detail and specific action.

It is usually a good idea to keep an event log, noting key actions and events. If you are deploying personnel to field locations it is essential to record their comings and goings so as not to lose track of individuals in potentially hazardous locations. Taking part in a field rescue operation is itself a hazardous undertaking so you need to be sure that the people deployed have the necessary skills, judgement, equipment and communications.

Finally, do your best to remain calm and remember that you are neither infallible nor superhuman. Do not be afraid to recognise an error while there is till time to correct it and remember that you will be more effective if occasionally you make time to eat, drink and, on extended episodes, sleep.

Chapter summary

- Emergency response benefits from advance planning but must have sufficient flexibility to respond to the entirely unexpected.

- A calm and well prepared leader is essential for the field response to most emergencies.

- Emergency and crisis plans can outline some of the main actions and priorities for 'expected' emergencies.

- The controller needs to have single-minded focus on the situation without distractions.

Chapter 12

Review and audit

Review and audit are two ways by which the quality and safety of an organisation can be monitored. Both aim to bring experienced specialists, who may be internal or external, into contact with all relevant aspects of the organisation's operation.

The terms tend to be used interchangeably but 'review' generally refers to an internal process that does not result in measurement against particular standards and 'audit' to a process undertaken by an external agency that makes decisions relative to a defined standard.

Internal review

The process of field observation by managers and other senior staff provides regular contact with course delivery and identifies problems at an early stage. Instructors themselves are usually keen to improve the safety and quality of what they do and their opinions, based on a privileged viewpoint of activities, are important.

Their willingness to communicate is enhanced in an open culture and also if they see that their comments are having an effect. It is important that safety concerns or adverse events are dealt with, but it is also important for staff to *see* that they are being dealt with. This needs attention from managers when a difficulty has been noted but the decision is taken that no further action, such as a change of practice, is necessary.

The process of incident recording and analysis described in Chapter 13 provides a hit list of the particular areas of concern at a given time. These are the issues that should be given priority attention.

Safety reviews

This is a system that was developed by Outward Bound® in North America and is now widely used. It has proved effective in:

- supporting and promoting the continuous improvement of safety standards;
- sharing best practice between individual operating units;
- identifying any uncontrolled hazards.

A safety review usually involves a team of external or quasi-external reviewers visiting an activity provider for several days, interviewing staff and participants, observing representative activities, systems and facilities and then reporting on their findings and recommendations. The review leader oversees and controls the process and usually has primary responsibility for preparing the final report and monitoring its follow up. Team members all agree the findings and recommendations.

The safety review process works best if the tone is a constructive one, aiding continuous improvement of the host organisation by a combination of audit and consultancy, but the atmosphere should not be too cosy. The process is costly of resources and should be expected to generate focused, detailed and relevant comment and recommendations, not uncritical approval.

As an example of scale and frequency, a UK Outward Bound® school (with a typical operational level of 35,000 activity days per annum) undergoes a biennial review with a team of three or four reviewers. For a newly established provider, or one where operational difficulties have been found on a previous visit, a one-year interval may be preferred, and it may be reasonable for smaller operations to use a smaller review team.

Safety reviews tend to be used mainly by larger organisations, but there is no doubt that smaller providers will benefit from a comparable approach. One aspect that makes the process a convenient one for large multi-site operations is the relative ease with which reviewers can be sourced from different operating units. Such people can combine both an external perspective and a useful level of general knowledge of the organisation being reviewed. They are also likely to identify useful ideas and effective practices that they can take back to their own part of the operation.

The areas that the review will usually address are wide ranging. If one starts to construct a network of the interacting systems and processes that influence the safe operation of even a small organisation, it will be found to be very extensive. As an example, the safe completion of a coastal sailing journey by an instructor and a group of trainees may depend on many factors including, among many others, the following:

- how the instructor and backup staff are recruited, trained and authorised;
- the experience and judgement of the supervisory staff;
- the methods of sourcing and acting on weather information;
- effective communication systems and emergency plans;
- the means by which plans are monitored and approved;
- appropriate sourcing, specification and maintenance of the vessel and its equipment;
- knowledge of the presence in participants of medical conditions such as asthma or epilepsy;
- how the organisation has learned from any previous problems with sailing journeys;
- the quality of clothing and personal safety equipment.

In addition, the arrangements need to have a sufficient margin of safety and sufficient flexibility to be able to accommodate the unexpected and unpredicted – adverse weather, illness, mechanical failure and so on. The advance identification of a 'Plan B' can assist this.

Combine this with similar lists for a range of other activities and it can be seen that a review might extend from equipment purchase to child protection policies and from climbing to catering arrangements.

To accommodate this range the team of safety reviewers will usually operate to a schedule identifying broad areas of interest or categories of investigation. This should reflect the priorities of the organisation commissioning the review but will typically include:

- participant preparation and screening;
- staff qualifications and training;
- management systems;
- programme activities;
- emergency procedures;
- food and equipment;
- facilities and security;
- transportation.

In turn, each of these will cover a number of subsidiary topics and these are usually presented as a series of questions, each of which will require considered answers from the review team, except when the occasional question is not applicable to the subject organisation. So, the category of 'emergency procedures' might include questions such as:

- Is there a written plan for emergency response to cover all reasonable eventualities?
- Are staff aware of its existence and location?
- Are the contact details of rescue agencies readily available to all staff?
- Is there a duty manager system and does this work effectively?
- Are staff and participants briefed on fire procedures?
- Are unaccompanied students adequately briefed on emergency procedures?
- Is first-aid equipment readily available during all activities and is it fit-for-purpose?
- Does the centre have a policy for dealing with disclosure, threats of self-harm and substance abuse? Is this appropriate? Are field staff aware of it?
- Have all field staff received training in child protection issues? Have support staff?
- Are night-duty staff appropriately trained and informed?

Typically, some important topics might be touched upon under several different headings, so fire procedures and evacuation plans might have produced comment under both 'emergency procedures' and 'facilities'. One of the tasks of the review team leader is to ensure that a coherent and integrated view is taken of these broader issues.

To learn about these areas the reviewers will:

- have briefings from senior management;
- make observations of as wide a range of representative activities as is possible;
- interview a representative selection of staff and participants.

Field staff are often the most knowledgeable about actual safety management practices. Developing relationships that will allow the reviewers to learn how staff operate is vital to conducting a well-informed review. Interviews with students and other staff can also be helpful.

Other typical activities include reviews of:

- planning procedures for new programme activities;
- staff files for evidence of current certifications, background checks and performance appraisals;
- accident and incident records;
- evaluation systems;
- equipment, facilities and vehicles;
- driver screening and training procedures;
- emergency action plans.

Reviewers should avoid inappropriate intrusion into the organisation's work and be ready to step back if their presence is having an adverse effect on a particular session. If staff and students have been properly briefed, they usually welcome reviewers.

The team leader is responsible for ensuring that all the review categories are covered. Regular regrouping of the review team is desirable. This allows team members to compare observations, discuss any issues or trends and allocate new assignments.

Team members should consider making written notes of their field observations. It is not necessary to observe an entire activity session to make worthwhile observations but the initial briefing and setting up of a session and its culminating minutes are often of great interest. It is useful for reviewers to have expertise and depth in the activities being observed but many valuable insights will come even from individuals who do not have this depth but simply an alert and questioning approach. When criticisms are made of some aspect of the work of the host centre it is vital that these are supported by evidence.

When a reviewer has been observing an activity it is often desirable to give instructors feedback covering positive features observed and constructive criticisms. Any major criticisms that an instructor may not be able to address should usually be communicated first to managers. Our primary interest is in the underlying systems and management arrangements rather than the performance of individual staff. Be aware that the presence of a reviewer can be very intimidating for the person being observed.

The remoteness of magnificent country like this adds an extra dimension to risk management.

Reviewers should take care to maintain a professional approach with:

- appropriate behaviour, dress and language;

- not taking over activities, even if the reviewer 'can do it better' than the staff;

- observing high standards of personal safety.

It is well for reviewers to remember above all that they are guests!

AALA

Licensing authority inspections audit the provider but this is constrained by time limits. The inspection is ultimately about whether the provider meets minimum acceptable standards which are defined by law, but the process has been enhanced by the fact that inspectors do give constructive advice to help all providers, even the best ones, to improve.

AALA inspections can be expected to throw up serious deficiencies in the provision but it is likely that more detailed and specific advice will emerge from a process that can commit more than a few hours to the task.

Accreditation

A number of other non-statutory accreditation schemes exist and these are of particular value for organisations who are beyond the scope of AALA inspections. The best ones usually have clearly defined standards, will have some process of inspection and will make recommendations, some mandatory, to providers applying for accreditation.

Chapter summary

- Processes of review and audit help to identify areas for improvement.
- Regular reviews support continuous improvement and sharing of good practice.
- It is desirable to combine the closeness of internal review with the objectivity of external review.
- Some audits, such as AALA inspections and Local Authority environmental health inspections, are mandatory for certain providers.

Chapter 13

Incident recording and analysis

It is surprising that there are outdoor organisations who appear to make no systematic effort to learn from incidents, unless the occurrence is of such gravity that some reaction is forced upon them.

An undeveloped view of adverse occurrences in adventure activities sees them as one-off, entirely atypical events arising from a combination of bad luck and very unusual circumstances. Even the word 'accident' carries this suggestion of chance misfortune. Some workers in other fields have suggested that the term be replaced by 'preventable occurrence', in order to promote the understanding that many 'accidents' are predictable and preventable and are only rarely genuinely random events.

We probably need to regard accidents and other such events as inevitable manifestations of the fact that we have imperfect control over some of the important variables (most notably people and the great outdoors) that affect what we do. As in any complex undertaking, we must expect that things will not always go to plan and that errors will occur, yet, at the same time, we can also utilise incidents as a rich seam of learning about our performance and how we might operate more effectively.

For large providers, becoming a learning organisation is the key to effective risk management in the long term. A pivotal process within such an organisation is that of identifying and reporting adverse occurrences, deciding their significance and, where necessary, modifying practice accordingly. If you wait for things to have gone seriously wrong before looking at what might be an area of vulnerability, you are dramatically hampering your ability to learn and improve.

The occurrence of accidents in all organisations tends to conform to a pyramid pattern (see Figure 13.1). At its pinnacle are serious incidents or fatalities, but these high-profile occurrences tend to rest on foundations built from much greater numbers of incidents of lesser impact. By collecting data on the incidents that are not life threatening, we get a much larger and more representative sample and are then much more likely to see patterns emerging. So minor incidents and, even more so, near misses, can give us vitally important lessons, often at little cost of injury or time.

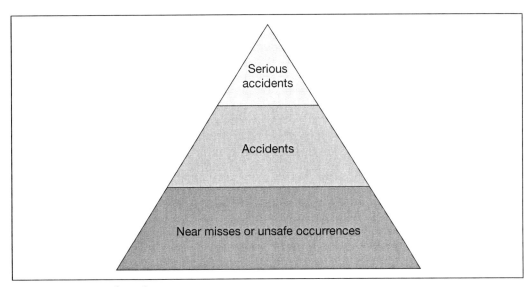

Figure 13.1 Pattern of accident occurrence.

The same principles apply to smaller organisations or individual leaders but because the opportunity to collect statistically useful data is more limited, there needs to be some proportionality of approach. Calculating the rate of occurrence of a certain type of incident may be a very illuminating exercise for an organisation with tens of thousands of participants each year; for a sole provider working with small numbers of clients, such a rate is probably not worth the effort of production and is likely to vary considerably from year to year. For small-scale operations it is worth considering whether it is possible to combine and compare reports with those of others in comparable positions. Thus it may not be practicable for an individual teacher to identify trends of adverse occurrences in his/her own work, but if that teacher's data is integrated into that for an entire education authority, then trends and patterns for the entire set of data readily emerge – and can, if fed back, inform the future work of individual teachers.

Various approaches are outlined below as an indication of what can be considered. The decision must be made as to what is an appropriate level of response for a particular provider. It might be useful to ask the questions:

- Are we confident that we know about all notable incidents?
- Do we hear about near misses?
- Do incidents in the past influence the way we will operate in the future?
- How do we communicate to our staff what we learn about incidents?

It will readily be seen that the answers to these questions are intimately bound up with the nature of the prevailing organisational culture as discussed in Chapter 4. Some of the information and analysis to be described is based on quantitative data, some on qualitative data.

An example of a qualitative statement would be: 'During the last few days there have been several near misses reported that have involved the discovery of discarded hypodermic needles in the parkland area used for lawn games'. Numerical analysis would add nothing to this important report – it hardly matters whether there have been two or twenty – it is already clear that urgent action is necessary. A quantitative statement might be 'During 5,200 student activity days, four incidents resulted in hospital visits'.

Quantitative analysis of incident data is a particularly powerful tool for larger organisations. Every operation can benefit from a qualitative examination of the data.

Incidents

I prefer to use the term 'incident' to describe adverse occurrences, largely to escape from the assumption that only accidents need concern us. Of course accidental injury should feature prominently but all of the following should be considered for inclusion in reporting:

- accidents;
- illnesses;
- near misses;
- behavioural incidents;
- pre-existing conditions.

Severity

It is often desirable to have additional options to indicate severity or seriousness so that one may report a minor illness, a significant accident or a serious behavioural incident. Some organisations use 'lost day cases' as an indicator of the more important accidents, these being occurrences that result in the loss of at least one day of programme activity after the day of injury or illness.

This method is widely used but there are potential difficulties in how one deals with a serious incident occurring on the last day of a course (and therefore not resulting in lost programme days) or when the instructor reporting does not yet know if lost days resulted. In addition, the criterion is context dependent. Someone feeling a little unwell on a residential programme could easily take a day out. On an extended journey, taking a day out may only be possible by entirely leaving the course. So the same condition can result in a lost day case or an 'early departure' for one student and not for the other.

Accidents

Accidental injury can encompass a huge range of conditions from minor cuts and grazes through to grave, life-threatening injury. It is usual to have some way of defining the lower limit of what is to be reported, such as any injury that requires medical attention or results in loss of participation time in activities. If this line is set too high, for example, by being confined to legally reportable injuries, then we are shrinking the base of our safety pyramid and many informative incidents will be omitted; if too low, we may have a distractingly large volume of what might be regarded as trivial occurrences.

When people are travelling in rugged terrain the most common forms of non-trivial accidental injury usually occur as a result of a slip or stumble and include ankle sprains and fractures, twisted knees and other lower limb injuries, closely followed by upper limb injuries such as wrist sprains and fractures and shoulder injuries.

Grave injury tends to arise as a result of drowning, falls from height, falling objects, fire, the effect of extremes of heat or cold and vehicle accidents.

Illnesses

This category tends mainly to cover physical illness although it is by no means uncommon for psychological illnesses to manifest themselves in the unusual circumstances of an outdoor programme. Minor headaches and gastro-intestinal conditions are probably the most common illnesses but the conditions that combine both potential seriousness and frequency of occurrence in the population are asthma, diabetes and epilepsy. Identifying those participants who suffer from these conditions is an important function of the medical screening described in Chapter 4. If the condition is well managed there are few occasions when sufferers cannot take part in the full range of adventurous activities. Medical advice is desirable in the more severe cases.

In the United Kingdom, asthma is a very common condition in school-age children and while its effects are often mild, rare cases can present a full-scale medical emergency necessitating urgent provision of oxygen and evacuation to hospital. Many sufferers will be prescribed inhalers to control the condition and those in charge of children so equipped will usually need to ensure ready access to the medication as needed.

People with diabetes often take supplementary insulin, a hormone that controls the metabolism of sugars, and will usually need to balance food intake with energy output. The physical demands of an outdoor course may be unusual and the diet unfamiliar, with the result that the balance of food intake and energy output can easily go awry. The most important form of imbalance is a rapid drop of blood sugar resulting initially in excitable behaviour, followed quite rapidly by drowsiness and eventual coma. Early treatment by giving any form of sugar by mouth has an immediate effect of reversal. It is worth noting that injectable insulin can become denatured if it is allowed to freeze – as might happen on a mountainside.

Epilepsy may present great difficulties of management in the case of individuals who are liable to sudden fits or absences. A sudden loss of consciousness on an exposed rocky section of a hill walk, when cycling in traffic, while swimming or during a kayak capsize can, in each case, have very severe consequences. Getting an indication of the likely frequency of attacks is an important aspect of screening and subsequent decisions about management may well require a greatly increased level of supervision by staff. It is generally unwise for an individual suffering frequent attacks to undertake a standard programme with standard staffing levels unless this consists of easily managed activities in forgiving environments.

Near misses

A 'near miss' can be defined as an event that, with small changes of circumstances, could have resulted in notable loss or injury, or an event that throws light on deficiencies in our risk management arrangements.

It is, of course, easy to reduce this to the absurd 'man walks down street and could have fallen over' kind of reporting. A useful principle is to exclude all 'minor' near misses on the basis that important information concerning notable loss or injury, or system defects, is expected to be present when a near miss is recorded.

Some events, such as a piece of heavy equipment crashing to the deck close to the crew of a sailing yacht are clearly 'near misses' but others will only be recognised by the alert and trained mind. Of huge value, and an indicator of high competence in staff, is the situation where an instructor or a manager recognises that an existing practice or set of conditions is intrinsically hazardous and is able to instigate defensive changes before any loss or injury occurs. Sometimes this emerges as part of normal good practice or overlaps with risk assessment such as when, with a landowner's permission, low tree branches overhanging a river and presenting a high water 'strainer' hazard to kayakers may be removed or loose rock on a climbing crag is cleaned under carefully controlled circumstances.

Spotting intrinsic weaknesses in systems is more difficult. The negative reporting, so notorious in the case of the Zeebrugge disaster, which operated on the assumption that 'if there was a problem, someone will tell us about it' is an example of a fundamental weakness that escaped identification by some highly skilled and experienced officers and crew. The external eye, as described in Chapter 12 in connection with safety reviews, is an important way of improving the likelihood that such system defects will be caught in time – and it is likely that every system will have flaws of some kind.

Some very serious incidents are entirely unpredictable and could not have been anticipated from incident data. If a student is hit by a meteorite we are hardly likely to find a catalogue of previous near misses signalling the hazard. However, the reality is that many serious events conform to a pattern that has occurred before, and is evident in the record of near misses or minor accidents, but where we were previously lucky enough for it not to result in serious injury. The unreported observations of near swamping of a sailing boat, described in Chapter 8, show how an opportunity can be missed in this area.

It is not uncommon, and perhaps understandable, that those immediately involved in tragic occurrences tend to attribute events to monstrous misfortune, a near impossible combination of circumstances, and to overlook any indications that might have previously signalled the possibility of loss. Those responsible for learning from such occurrences should take care to look beneath the surface of events.

I sympathise with the often voiced opinion that 'near miss' is a slightly unfortunate term, that it suggests, inaccurately, that we lurch from one uncontrolled event to another, but it is in such wide use that there is, in my view, little to be gained by substituting 'near accident', 'unsafe occurrence' or some other term.

One of the vital requirements of effective reporting of all incidents, and especially of near misses, is an open culture where people are willing to report. Reports should be treated in a way that encourages staff to continue reporting! This does not happen overnight and senior staff need to work hard to establish it. You are in a healthy culture when staff are even willing to report incidents that show themselves in a poor light.

Behavioural incidents

This category can include aggressive and disruptive behaviour, assaults, bullying, use of illegal substances and alcohol misuse. At its most serious, it can cover assaults and overdoses that are life-threatening. Any malicious assault has a shocking character that can have an impact far beyond the immediate injuries incurred; even purely verbal assaults can represent an attack on the self that may haunt the victim for years.

Some cultures view alcohol misuse as a bit of a joke but in an outdoor context, alcohol-fuelled irrational behaviour can have serious consequences. Anybody that has used alcohol or other substances to the point where they lose consciousness is in a most vulnerable state, with a severely threatened airway that is likely to require supervisory care. Such occurrences should be given appropriate importance in reporting.

Pre-existing conditions

Many people will attend an outdoor event when they are already suffering from an injury or other condition If an old knee injury flares up during a mountain expedition it is appropriate to record this as a pre-existing condition or aggravated injury.

Data collection

Having decided on the types of incident to be recorded a method of data gathering has to be chosen. A standard pro forma has much to commend it; it is convenient, acts as an *aide-mémoire* to those reporting and provides an immediate documentary record. Once a moderate volume of data exists its compilation into a computer database generates a resource that becomes more valuable with each passing year.

Other Information

It is obvious that the report should identify:

- the person who is the subject of the report;
- the person making the report (often the instructor in charge at the time of occurrence);
- the date, time and place of the incident;
- any injuries sustained;
- the activity being undertaken at the time of occurrence;
- the responsible organisation;
- the type of course or event;
- the seriousness of the incident;
- any immediate medical treatment given.

It is also useful for a responsible person to be able to sign off that the report has been received and to indicate any consequent action or recommendations. Some organisations record lost day cases.

Damage to property

It may be considered desirable to record occasions where equipment, facilities or vehicles are lost or damaged. I prefer to use for this a process separate from the standard reporting of incidents, except when the damage has a clear influence on the safety of staff and participants, as would be the case with vehicle collisions or damage to safety equipment.

If it is decided to use a single form of reporting it is wise to prevent the analysis of safety issues being distorted by large quantities of data from property events.

Analysis

There is a basic housekeeping need to collect incident data as a simple record but, beyond this, the ability of organisations and individuals to learn from incidents is strongly affected by how this data is analysed and how the resultant insights are disseminated.

Pattern of distribution by type

It is useful to have a sense of the breakdown of incidents in your organisation into the different types. This can illuminate the future management of operations. As an example, Figure 13.2 shows the breakdown of a year's tally of all reported incidents in a large outdoor organisation working primarily with young people.

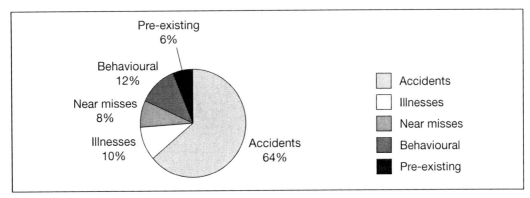

Figure 13.2 Incident types – all incidents

If we confine the analysis just to 'notable' incidents (arbitrarily, those identified as 'significant' or 'serious' but omitting 'minor') a somewhat different distribution is evident, as seen in Figure 13.3.

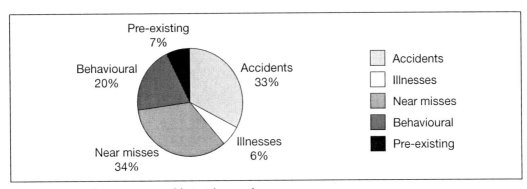

Figure 13.3 Incident types – notable incidents only.

The percentage of accidents has declined considerably in the second chart and both behavioural and near miss occurrences have strongly increased. It is likely that minor injuries, such as twisted ankles, dominate the data for all incidents and these are absent in the second chart. Near misses, should by definition, be important so these feature strongly. The indication is that when behavioural incidents are recorded, they tend to be of an important nature.

It is important to remember that, although of great value to the learning organisation, near misses do not, of themselves, put people in hospital so, to that extent, are of less pressing importance than the incidents that might so do.

For completeness, if the same data is confined only to 'serious' incidents, the pattern in Figure 13.4 emerges.

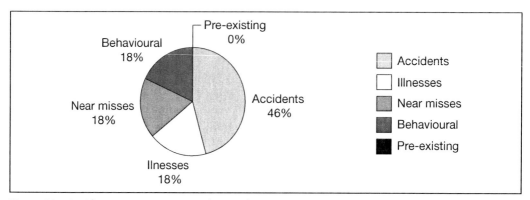

Figure 13.4 Incident types – serious incidents only.

However, it is important to note that, at this level of analysis, we have a small sample of just 11 incidents, which is therefore of limited statistical significance. Because of this, we would expect this particular pie chart for serious incidents to show considerable variation from year to year.

The accidents considered here in fact include two broken ankles, both arising when participants were running in a domestic context, and two injuries, fortunately minor, arising from a vehicle collision where a third party was judged responsible.

Pattern of distribution by activity

Everybody involved in adventure activities knows that some activities are more likely to generate incidents than others. However, the facts can be surprising and it is not uncommon to find that some of the more spectacular high challenge activities have a relatively low level of incident occurrence while other, apparently innocuous ones, produce frequent injuries.

One large outdoor centre found that the most likely cause of notable injury to participants was not sailing, kayaking, ropes courses or climbing but informal football sessions played in snatched minutes either side of meals. Learning this allowed steps to be taken to reduce this occurrence. This illustrates why some analysis by activity is desirable.

Figure 13.5 provides an analysis of the same data set as that used for Figures 13.2 to 13.4 above on incidents by type but with the notable incidents broken down by activity.

Dynamics is a jargon term referring to problem-solving exercises. It is noticeable how non-programme activities (the football mentioned above is a good example) are the largest sector. On this evidence it is important to put considerable effort into managing this 'down time' of participants.

To ensure that unsupported inferences are not drawn, it is always necessary to approach the analysis of data with some caution. There is a certain crudeness in any process that reduces a complex event to a written record, and particularly so if the data is kept in a concise form.

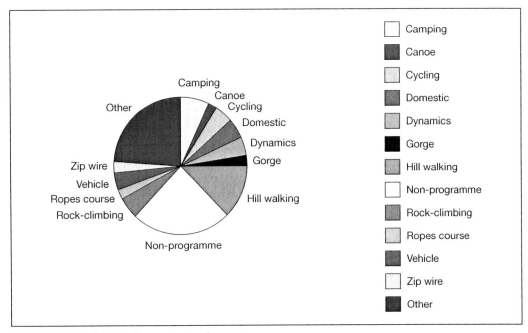

Figure 13.5 Notable incident occurence by activity.

Something to note with this kind of data is the fact that a wide variety of incident types may be recorded under a single activity heading, so that, by way of example, rock climbing incidents could include;

- a slip during the approach to the crag resulting in a sprained ankle;

- equipment failure;

- an assault by one participant on another;

- an asthma attack;

- a near miss by a falling rock;

- the recurrence of a back strain;

- failure by a belayer to hold a fall.

For several of these, it is purely incidental that the activity in progress at the time of occurrence was rock climbing. For this reason it is important to take a general overview of the data before concluding, for example, that rock climbing is a terribly dangerous activity.

Overview

This crucial process tasks an experienced person or persons with scanning the data for incidents of particular importance that may not have emerged from a more statistical approach. This is an important aspect of the use of qualitative data and is often the point at which some reclassification is desirable. A multiple kayak capsize in a sheltered bay on a summer day is probably a minor incident but the same occurrence in the cold water of March may deserve a 'significant' or 'serious' rating.

Another useful method is to identify the five or ten most important incidents for the period under analysis and to decide whether any changes of operational practice are needed. These headline issues can be part of the process of dissemination and may be all that is needed for a small organisation.

Use of databases

When a system of incident recording has been devised, a logical extension is to summarise data on a computer database using the key data as recorded on the reporting form. This allows rapid access to the summary data and easy analysis. The cumulative data that is collected becomes of increasing value as a management tool with each passing year as the size of the data expands. Outward Bound Trust is now able to call on data from over one million activity days for their own courses. Figure 13.6 provides an example of an entry.

ID	DATE	CENTRE	ACTIVITY	INCIDENT	INJURY	SIGNIFICANCE	NATURE	IMMEDIATE CAUSE
84	29/03/2002	WAL	HILLWALK	Slipped in stream	Cut lip	MINOR	ACCIDENT	FALL/SLIP

LOST DAYS	WORK AREA	ACCOMP?	AGE	M/F	STAFF	COMMENT
0	OTHER	Yes	14	F	No	

Figure 13.6 Example of entry in the Outward Bound Trust database.

Figure 13.6 is a representation in summary form of an incident where, during a hill-walking expedition, a 14-year-old female slipped while crossing a stream and sustained a cut lip. An instructor was accompanying the group at the time of the injury which did not result in any programme days being lost. It was considered to be of minor importance.

The most useful feature of putting such information on a database is the ability to sort data by different categories. Thus, if we are concerned about the management arrangements for a particular activity or want to set an adverse event in a wider context, it is the work of a few minutes to list the relevant previous occurrences.

If, for example, a suggestion to introduce the use of helmets for flat water canoeing is under consideration, then finding out whether there have previously been any head injuries in the activity is easily accomplished. The final decision may depend on other factors such as public expectations or standard industry practice but some hard facts usually help to illuminate debate. (One would, of course, expect that any notable occurrence of head injury in the activity would have already been identified and acted upon.)

The database is only as useful as the data it contains and so can make no useful prediction of the occurrence of completely new kinds of incidents, but the use of sequential sorting by different variables allows the user to identify all incidents at a particular site, all camping incidents at a particular site, all staff incidents across all sites and so on.

Dissemination

Data collection and analysis can become a sterile, academic exercise if the lessons drawn are not communicated back to those involved in field operations in a way that can positively influence future activity. Some people are adept at the analysis of graphs and charts, others prefer a narrative presentation of data, so it is worth using parallel methods and to make the message match the requirements of the recipient.

The headline data described above is a good starting point for all those concerned with the delivery of activities. A more comprehensive approach is to compile a digest of important incidents. This is selective, concentrating on those incidents from which some useful lessons can be drawn. Here are some extracts from such a document, which also include comments by the editor (bulleted):

Fuel bottles inadequately marked

Member of an expedition group had brought his own petrol type fuel for a specialist MSR stove. This became mixed up with the methylated alcohol fuel for the standard Trangia stove in use by other participants. The confusion was identified before any dangerous occurrence.

Trapped foot between wall and boulder

Young male trapped foot whilst in waist deep moving water. Freeing it was difficult.

- *A serious problem in faster or higher water.*

Student pinned between boats

Student having difficulty paddling in fairly strong tidal stream was carried onto moored inflatable boats and pinned. Rapidly rescued by staff and resumed activity.

● *This hazard had been anticipated but not prevented.*

Group split up on hill

Group, 14 years old, disobeyed instructions during an unaccompanied walk and split up following a dispute.

Fell down drop in cave after removing glasses

M 15 removed his glasses and so failed to see a short drop. He fell forward but was fortunately uninjured.

● *People who can only see adequately when wearing spectacles are at a considerable disadvantage in wet, muddy conditions and when there is distracting reflected light – hence their removal.*

Decorators set a window on fire

Decorators stripping paint from an old window frame ignited rotten wood. Smoke was spotted by kitchen staff. Extinguishing the fire was made more difficult because the window was jammed and the external face was covered in a protective metal screen.

Boulder loosened by higher member of group

M 14 struck by boulder knocked off by colleague further up hill.

● *Was party management appropriate?*

It is normal to subdivide the digest into sections on canoeing, sailing, walking and so on. Everybody involved in the provision of programme activities or residential support should have the opportunity to see the digest, which can usefully be issued on an annual or biennial basis.

For incidents of wide relevance a narrative summary of the salient facts can be widely distributed as an indicator of 'lessons learned'. Some high-profile outdoor accidents, such as that at Stainforth Beck, have received this treatment in the UK and the Marine Accident Investigation Branch (MAIB) have a statutory duty to do this for accidents at sea. Although few of the latter's reports originate in the recreational or educational sectors, the regular digests published by MAIB make illuminating reading to anyone interested in the dynamics of error and misfortune. Elsewhere, the National Outdoor Leadership School (NOLS) in the US publish digests of incidents and, in a more specialised field, the Canadian Avalanche Association publishes an analysis of collected incidents in a presentation of exemplary clarity.

Numerical analysis

A further example of a statement based on quantitative data is 'the rate of occurrence of notable incidents in 2005 is 1.5 per 1,000 participant activity days'. This statement means that, on average, there have been about 1.5 reports of incidents of note for every 1,000 activity days. If we express the same data in a different way, and project similar performance into the future, we can predict that, if an average instructor works with a group of 10 students, then that instructor can expect, on average, to report one incident of note every 66 days that they are in charge of a group (1,000/1.5 × 10 = 66 approximately).

Small organisations have a lesser need of numerical analysis of incident data because the sample size is too small to be statistically reliable. In any case, one should beware of reading more into quantitative data than is actually there. Although the example given above appears to be an unarguable and clear statement of fact, it is actually built on a number of assumptions or variable criteria including the propensity of staff to report and the subjective nature of classification, such as the definition of 'notable incidents'. Other external factors can influence the data and these need to be considered if comparisons are to be made between different organisations, different sites or different instructors.

What quantitative analysis can usefully do is to give an indication of rates of occurrence that then permit annual comparisons and the identification of any underlying trends. This is of particular value for larger organisations, where there is sufficient data to allow meaningful year-on-year comparisons. Trends are possibly more informative than absolute levels. A reporting unit that shows year-on-year deterioration in the incident rate may need to look carefully at what might be the root causes of this alarming signal.

In order to avoid awkward numbers it is normal to express rates against a base of one thousand activity days, so that one might quote a lost day case (LDC) rate of 1.2 per one thousand activity days. This is a typical value and means that, on average, slightly more than one LDC occurs every one thousand activity days. This measure is a convenient way of defining more serious occurrences since any incident that results in the subject missing one or more programme days (other than the day of the incident) is recorded as an LDC. It has the disadvantage of excluding near misses, or important incidents that have not resulted in lost programme days, and also requires some kind of protocol to deal with incidents occurring on the final day of a course.

I find it useful to work out the rate of recording of near misses and regard this as a quick way of taking the pulse of the organisation regarding its openness and willingness to report. A good level of recording of near misses suggests that there is an open reporting culture and that staff are sufficiently aware to be able successfully to identify near misses.

The most relevant data for comparison between activities is to compare rates of occurrence in each activity. The data can be laborious to obtain since it requires us to record each day that a particular activity is provided.

When we start recording data and rates it seems obvious that we should aim to reduce these rates to the lowest level, but this is not necessarily the case. We are certainly trying to reduce the rate of occurrence of unnecessary injury but if too much emphasis is given to rates and incident totals it can have the undesirable effect of discouraging open reporting, reducing the learning that can be extracted and, in some cases, promoting inappropriate activity.

The business guru W.E. Deming describes a case where a large American manufacturing corporation put huge pressure on its site managers to reduce factory injury rates by tying this target into their personal performance bonuses. The site managers knew how they were to be measured and, sure enough, managed to achieve significant reductions in recorded injuries. Further investigation revealed that managers had done this by identifying the most dangerous processes and outsourcing these to a subcontractor, so that the accidents, which continued to happen, were not recorded in the plant's data. The board were, on this occasion, frustrated in their intention of improving real levels of safety.

Safety in adventure activities should not be a matter of presentation but should involve each one of us with unlimited personal responsibility. An honest approach and a wide view balancing the many relevant factors are most likely to deliver this. Numerical analysis of data contributes important information to this process.

Incident investigation

Incidents of special gravity may require further investigation. Normally, a senior person will be expected to decide if an investigation should be undertaken and, if so initiated, in what form. Sometimes the cause and circumstances of the incident are so clear that an investigation may be deemed unnecessary, but the preparation of a detailed written report will usually be desirable in order to disseminate information. When an investigation is instigated, a suitably qualified individual may be tasked with its completion or an investigating team may be brought together. For the most serious incidents the team may include, or entirely comprise, individuals external to the organisation being investigated.

Part of the response to an emergency should be to start the collection of information through the maintenance of a log and the retention of material such as:

- photographs at the scene of the incident;
- copies of weather forecasts;
- diagrams, sketches and maps of the event;
- a record of conditions at the site;
- critical equipment in use – which should be quarantined pending inspection;
- names of all personnel;
- initial witness statements;
- transcripts of key messages.

It is very common for people at the incident scene to 'tidy up' and inadvertently destroy valuable information. As long as it does not impede rescue efforts, equipment should where possible be undisturbed until a skilled person is able to inspect it, or until it can be photographed or otherwise recorded.

Once the phase of emergency response is completed a more detailed investigation may be considered and this may be done for incidents that did not originally stimulate an emergency response.

The primary purpose of an investigation is:

- To gather information on the circumstances of the incident;
- To analyse the facts;
- To establish a cause;
- To make recommendations, where appropriate, to prevent recurrence.

Chapter summary

- The recording and analysis of incident data is a powerful aid to learning and improvement.
- Incidents can include accidents, illnesses, near misses, behavioural incidents and pre-existing conditions.
- The occurrence of accidents tends to conform to a pyramid pattern.
- Data can be analysed and disseminated in both a qualitative (narrative) form or a numerical form.
- Numerical analysis tends to be most valuable in identifying trends in larger organisations.
- Incident investigation is a systematic response to a serious occurrence.

Chapter 14

The law

When the priorities of risk management in adventure activities are discussed it is often unclear whether, primarily, we are managing the immediate risks to participants and staff or the different risks arising from potential litigation and adverse publicity.

Some operators place excessive importance on the threat of litigation and pay less attention to direct management of the actual hazards that lead to accident, to injury and, ultimately, to adverse organisational consequences. Huge volumes of paper detailing procedures and processes are amassed that may have little influence on practical operations. Chapter 6 describes how this phenomenon shows itself in the production of risk assessments.

Of course, it is both important and rational for providers to consider the risks of litigation and loss of reputation; my complaint is that, in many quarters, we have the wrong prioritisation – the tail is in danger of wagging the dog.

Surely, most of our energies and resources should be focused on managing the risks directly associated with the delivery of adventure experiences. If we take proper care of the safety of staff and participants then most of the threats of litigation are defused. A very effective defence against charges of unlawful killing is to ensure that nobody dies in the first place.

In addition, there is a moral duty of care towards the safety of participants and staff that outweighs local legal definitions or the likelihood of litigation. It is often said that personal injury claims are much more frequent in Britain and the United States than elsewhere and my visits to adventure programmes in South Africa, Scandinavia, Eastern Europe and Asia tend to confirm that such claims are less prominent in the views of managers. A reduced fear of litigation is, of course, no justification for lesser standards of operation and for a widely provided activity such as canoeing or climbing, it is not difficult to identify the key features of good practice that would apply equally in Cornwall or Cape Province. An international provider should aspire to directly comparable standards of provision at all locations even though limited resources in developing countries can render this difficult. It is useful to understand some of the main features of the legal system and how these might affect our work in adventure activities.

The courts

There are fundamental differences between the legal systems in England and Scotland, and every other country has its own unique legal principles and processes. However, distinctions will usually be drawn between the equivalents of civil, criminal and coroners' courts, although they may well be given names different to these.

Civil courts

Civil courts exist to resolve disagreements between individuals or companies about whether rights have been infringed or obligations not carried out. Awards will often, but not always, involve money. The court is not empowered to give any custodial sentence. The great majority of legal actions relating to adventure activities take place in the civil courts.

An imaginary example would be a claim for the award of compensatory financial damages when an individual had sustained a fractured leg during a fall on an introductory skiing course. The resulting injury did not prosper and permanent disability seems to be likely.

The claim may be directed towards any person or company that is considered negligent, so may, in this example, include any or all of the following:

- the ski instructor (whose decision to use a particularly icy slope may be called into question);
- the holiday company (if their advertising – 'an ideal beginners' area' was considered to be misleading);
- the manufacturer of the ski binding (if the design and performance of the binding are considered inadequate);
- the ski technician who fitted and adjusted the binding (and may be considered to have done this incorrectly);
- the ski patroller who splinted the injury and evacuated the casualty to medical care (ditto);
- the doctor who treated the injury in hospital (ditto);
- the hospital in which that doctor operated (where facilities or practices are judged inadequate to treat the injury in question).

And so on. In reality, it is normal for the claim to be confined to the defendants against whom the action is both most likely to be successful and who are most likely to be able to pay any damages. A large claim against a defendant who has neither assets nor insurance is likely to be avoided.

The claimant's legal representatives will enter a claim through the court, the defendant or defendants will be informed and then each side will start to collect evidence to support their respective positions. This can be a slow process, not uncommonly measured in years. Its ultimate destination is the court trial, where the judge, or judge and jury, hear evidence from witnesses in order to decide the merits of the case of each party and then allocate costs and damages accordingly.

In many cases, after negotiation, the legal representatives of both claimant and defendant will agree to a mutually acceptable settlement without proceeding to the considerable expense, and uncertainty of outcome, of a court appearance.

Criminal court

In simple terms, criminal law deals with illegal acts, which the state punishes. It is rare for criminal charges to be brought in relation to adventure activities, but this has occurred after particularly serious incidents involving loss of life, when charges of manslaughter (unlawful killing) have been brought against those who were in a position of responsibility. Such events are extremely rare but have a chilling significance.

In England, the process of a criminal court is, as in the civil court, an adversarial one with two opposing parties. One party is always the state, conventionally represented in Britain by the monarch. A higher standard of proof pertains in criminal courts, being 'beyond reasonable doubt' as compared with the 'on the balance of probability' of civil courts. This is appropriate, since the court may impose not only a fine but also a custodial sentence, depriving a convicted person of their liberty and burdening them with a criminal record.

In a criminal court one is faced with the full majesty of the law. It is sobering to consider that serious departures from good practice on a river or mountain can result in an instructor or a voluntary leader standing to face grave charges in such a court.

In March 1993, four teenagers on an adventure programme died in the cold waters of Lyme Bay off the south coast of England when a kayak journey went tragically wrong. The managing director of the company that ran the activity centre was convicted of corporate manslaughter and imprisoned for three years.

Such a charge is unusual in Britain and indicates the seriousness with which these events were viewed. A particularly telling piece of evidence during the trial was the fact that, some months before the tragedy, two instructors had warned the centre manager that safety arrangements at the centre were inadequate. This warning had not been acted on. The law may regard a danger ignored as more damning than a danger unidentified. Corporate manslaughter can only exist when there is a 'controlling mind' with overall responsibility and control.

A former scout leader charged with the manslaughter of a 10-year-old boy who fell from the East Ridge of Snowdon in the autumn of 1999 was found not guilty by the jury at his trial in Caernarfon.

A teacher at a Lancashire school was sentenced to 12 months in prison following the death of a 10-year-old boy during a plunge pooling session, which had the members of the group jumping into a pool in Glenridding Beck, a mountain stream draining into Ullswater.

The teacher pleaded guilty to manslaughter, and is probably the first teacher to be sentenced for negligence on a school trip. It is noteworthy that the boy who drowned was not a pupil at the teacher's school but was the son of an assistant accompanying the visit.

Some of the important issues in this case were:

- the decision to conduct the activity in conditions of unusually high water levels and rapid flow;
- the unavailability of a rescue rope;
- the low water temperature, which both reduced survival time and the ability of those attempting rescue to operate effectively.

These types of cases attract considerable attention and tend to have a direct effect on public policy. The Lyme Bay incident and trial led to the establishment of the Adventure Activities Licensing Authority (AALA). The Glenridding Beck incident, together with a comparable incident at Stainforth Beck in which two schoolgirls drowned, led to the Department for Education and Skills (DfES) recommending the appointment of Educational Visit Coordinators in schools with a responsibility to give advice and provide vetting on school visits.

Coroners' courts

Coroners' courts have a restricted function and exist primarily to determine, in the case of a death reported to them, the identity of the deceased person and when, where and how the death occurred. They only operate when death has occurred, do not allocate damages or resolve disputes and do not allocate blame. In Scotland their equivalent is the Fatal Accident Inquiry. The inquest is an inquisitorial process, seeking to answer questions of fact, and not an adversarial one.

When a fatal accident has occurred in adventure activities, the death may be reported to the coroner. This was the case with the Stainforth Beck incident mentioned above.

Liability

To be successful in a civil claim, claimants must demonstrate that:

- a duty of care existed;
- the holder was negligent in discharging the duty;
- actual loss or damage occurred as a result of the breach.

Duty of care

It is obvious that professional and qualified instructors and leaders have a duty of care towards those in their charge and, as described in Chapter 7, the Health and Safety at Work Act 1974 makes it clear that employers and self-employed persons have a duty of care towards their employees and others affected by their activities, including any clients.

However, the law recognises a more general duty of care owed by any individual to those who are close enough to be directly affected by that individual's actions. Thus, if I am throwing stones into a river in which other people are swimming and a swimmer is injured by one of the projectiles, my actions are likely to be in breach of this general duty of care.

Any person who takes responsibility for minors (in Britain, those under 18 years of age) has a special duty of care in that they are expected to act in a manner similar to that which could be expected from a normally prudent parent – we are *in loco parentis*.

Duty of care is also affected by the context and circumstances in which it applies. We are expected to give a higher degree of care to individuals who are

In loco parentis. A friendly rapport is essential with younger children.

infirm or evidently more vulnerable. An example of this would be a novice in an adventure activity. A first-time sailor under instruction on a cruising yacht would require closer supervision, more careful briefing and, in certain conditions, more direct security from lifelines or personal buoyancy than an experienced crew member, the latter being regarded as more able to make their own decisions and less likely to get into trouble.

Negligence

It is a common and misguided belief that if something goes wrong, negligence can automatically be assumed to have existed. It can readily be seen that what are often described as 'Acts of God' can wreak havoc without any individual having been negligent. What is less clear, and to an extent counter-intuitive, is the fact that in eyes of the English courts, errors of judgement do not necessarily amount to negligence. Fortunately, there is no large body of case law relating to adventure activities but the same principles apply as do in the much more frequent cases of alleged medical negligence.

In 1968, Lord Denning commented on a case which related to medical negligence:

> A doctor is not to be held negligent simply because something goes wrong ...
> He is not liable for mischance, or misadventure. Nor is he liable for an error of judgement ...
> He is only liable if he falls below the standard of a reasonably competent practitioner in his field – *so much so* that his conduct may fairly be held to be – I will not say deserving of censure, but, at any rate, *inexcusable*. (*Hucks* v. *Cole* (1968))

This draws our attention to the importance of comparing the actions and decision of a responsible person to the body of opinion regarding good practice that exists among comparable professionals. In another, earlier, case the judge's directions to the jury in the case *Bolam* v. *Friern Hospital Management Committee* included the remarks:

> ... he is not guilty of negligence if he has acted in accordance with a practice accepted as proper by a responsible body of medical men skilled in that particular art ... Putting it the other way round, a man is not negligent, if he is acting in accordance with such a practice, merely because there is a body of opinion who would take a contrary view.

I interpret these as telling me that, when operating in a position of responsibility such as leader of an outdoor activity, I should take care to operate in a way that is consistent with the approach that would be taken by a substantial body of competent professionals in the same field.

Imagine that a climbing instructor chose to use a particular arrangement of ropes to protect his or her clients. If one of the clients had slipped and fallen as a result of a failure of this rope arrangement, then any subsequent litigation would undoubtedly focus upon whether the instructor had been negligent to use it.

The court would seek expert opinion and, if there was near universal condemnation by other mountaineering professionals of the rope system in use, then it would be hard to defend a charge

Abseil descent from the Inaccessible Pinnacle.

of negligence. Conversely, if the body of competent professionals took a view that, in a similar situation, they too would have used the same rope system, then a charge of negligence with respect to the choice to use that particular rope system would be difficult to sustain, even though it may be demonstrated that the rope arrangements were the cause of the injury. It is perhaps unlikely, but certainly not impossible, that large numbers of professionals would support a fundamentally flawed method, unless the flaws had, until that time, been unrecognised.

An interesting situation applies when competent opinion is divided. In the example given, if 60 per cent of comparable professionals judged the rope system to be unsuitable, as long as a substantial proportion (let us, for simplicity, say 40 per cent) thought it acceptable, then the fact alone that significant, indeed majority, professional opinion disagreed with the chosen practice does not, of itself, make that practice negligent.

This emphasises the importance of staying in touch with best practice, through contact with other professionals, with national governing bodies of activities and with guidance from outdoor education advisers, the DfES and AALA. If you are operating as a leader or instructor in a way that is consistent with advice from such bodies your legal vulnerability in the event of things going badly wrong is greatly reduced.

Actual loss or damage

This is probably the most obvious aspect, and avoiding actual loss or damage is, of course, prominent in the process of risk management. It does mean that any claimant has to demonstrate that loss or damage has occurred. Poor practice that does not result in loss or damage of some kind may be deplorable but will not lead to a successful claim for negligence.

Disclaimers and waivers

Disclaimers and waivers seek to modify the risk contract between the provider and the client. Disclaimers are unilateral statements by the provider, waivers are an undertaking by the client to give up certain rights. 'A waiver asks you to wave goodbye to your rights.'

The status of disclaimers varies with different legal codes. In Britain, the signing of a disclaimer or a waiver generally has little effect in reducing the liability of a person or company who has acted negligently or, in the event of a claim, reducing the rights of the person who signed it. In other countries, such as the USA and Canada, the disclaimer, if accepted, does appear to modify the legal responsibilities of the provider and the legal rights of the client.

Potential clients of adventure providers should read carefully any disclaimers or waivers and ask themselves if they really want to do business with providers who seem to ask clients to give up their rights to an unreasonable degree.

What reputable providers should do is to try to make it clear to clients what types of risk apply to the proposed activity and what level of residual risk remains beyond their control. Bland statements that 'safety is paramount' are valueless if the client does not really understand what level of actual risk is entailed.

A graphic example of a waiver that does not mince its words is the one produced by Canadian Mountain Holidays (CMH), a leading company in the field of helicopter skiing – a tremendously exciting and spectacular activity, but one with a significant level of residual risk. No potential client could possibly read the CMH waiver that they are asked to sign before enrolling and still believe that they are entering into an activity that is as safe and controllable as a walk in the park. Here is a short extract:

> I am aware of the risks inherent in skiing and I am aware that helicopter skiing has certain additional dangers and risks, including:
>
> AVALANCHES: I am aware that avalanches frequently occur in the mountainous terrain used for helicopter skiing and that avalanches have caused a number of fatalities involving heli-skiing ... I am aware that the risk of an avalanche is always present in helicopter skiing, that this risk cannot be completely eliminated by CMH ...

and so on.

Acknowledgement of risk

Some mountain guides in the Alps include a statement like this in their booking materials:

> Whilst I will make every effort to ensure their safety and enjoyment, clients must accept some responsibility for their own safety and recognise that certain hazards in the mountain environment might be beyond the control of the guide. The level of these hazards will vary according to the planned route. Please contact me if you require specific advice on this.

Some ascents, such as that of Mont Blanc, entail a higher level of residual risk than the norm. The standard ascent from the French side, by the Gouter Route, involves the crossing of the Grand Couloir, a shallow gully that funnels any falling stones from a large area above. This crossing cannot be avoided in any realistic way, and many people attempt it. Occasionally, people are hit by falling stones, sometimes with serious consequences. The guide can reduce the level of hazard by choosing a suitable time of crossing, insisting that everyone wears helmets and by traversing the gully in an efficient and alert manner, but the hazard cannot be completely eliminated. The only way to entirely eliminate the hazard of the Grand Couloir is to go elsewhere, so any would-be summiteer has to balance the risk against the benefit – which takes us back to the issues discussed in Chapters 1 and 2.

At the upper end of challenge. A voluntary simulation of sudden immersion in a frozen lake.

In my opinion, the ethical and professional position of the guide is enhanced if clients understand this situation and the limits of the guide's control.

Wet Feet Limited

We have more than twenty years' experience in providing adventurous activities and consider our safety arrangements to be of a high standard. To learn more visit our website.

The risk of serious injury to participants is extremely small but it is not non-existent. We take a great deal of care over participants' safety, but, as in any adventure activity, there will be some factors beyond our control.

Participants will be briefed before every activity, are expected follow the safety procedures explained to them and also to indicate if they are unsure of what is expected of them. *Participants are never forced to do an activity and if any participant has concerns they should make these known to their instructor.*

The level of risk associated with Wet Feet Limited activities is normally very low, and probably no greater than that experienced by active people in everyday life. Most courses will include elements of:

Rough terrain such as rough vegetation, boulder fields and forests.

Physical effort, such as uphill walking carrying rucksacks. However, the pace of the group is determined by the slowest member and high levels of fitness are not necessary.

Water as part of canoeing, sailing or other activities. Appropriate safety measures are used. The ability to swim is not a requirement.

Height – operating above ground level during climbing or other activities. Appropriate safety measures are used.

Weather and climate. We are an outdoor organisation so the nature of the environment in which we operate is not always controllable. Even with good equipment, people may, at times, be cold and wet.

I understand and accept the above:

Signature of Participant, Parent or Guardian

Signing this does not release Wet Feet Limited from any of its legal obligations and does not diminish your legal rights.

Figure 14.1 Example of an acknowledgement of risk.

These are examples from unusually challenging activities targeted at adults, but the same principles apply widely. When a parent is trying to decide whether to give consent for their child to go camping or mountain biking or hill walking, the provider of these activities should make efforts to ensure that this consent is *informed* consent by explaining what the child will actually be doing and what the level of risk is expected to be. Many providers have staff who live and breathe sailing or kayaking and it is easy for them to assume that the rest of the world shares their enthusiasm and their detailed knowledge of the activity.

Each provider should think about what clients and parents should know. Figure 14.1 provides an imaginary example. Some will feel it goes too far, others not far enough.

Chapter summary

- The best defence against legal action is to operate with care and in line with accepted good practice.
- Adventure activities may fall within the jurisdiction of the civil, criminal or coroners' courts.
- To establish liability the claimant must show that:
  - a duty of care existed;174
  - there was negligence in discharging this duty;
  - actual loss or damage occurred as a result of the breach.
- Actions contrary to those considered appropriate by a large body of professionals in the field may be considered negligent.
- An acknowledgement of risk helps to clarify the level of risk that the provider knows to exist.

Chapter 15

International aspects

The need for rites of passage – testing experiences of self-realisation for youngsters on the verge of adulthood – may be as old as humankind and certain teachers have always used the powerful combination of the inspiration of nature and the illumination of experiential learning. It is therefore not surprising that adventure education is a worldwide phenomenon, although it is certainly arguable that, in less economically developed countries, life itself contains enough uncertainty and challenge to render unnecessary the more esoteric forms of outdoor education.

The range of provision

There are considerable variations of scale and type of provision. The United States, Canada, the UK, New Zealand and Australia all have a wealth of programmes, perhaps because much of the literature and early development of outdoor education has been in the Anglophone countries. In those countries, the use of outdoor excursions as a complement to classroom learning is well established and most, but by no means all, youngsters will have an opportunity for some kind of experience of education through an adventure sport.

Although in many countries the opportunities for adventure education are restricted, each will have some provision. A spectrum of providers exists between those who 'let the mountains speak for themselves' through to those who have highly developed regimes of facilitation and review, but all are united in the view that a special kind of learning takes place.

Some countries focus attention squarely on competence in an activity with personal development as a welcome by product. In Switzerland, adolescents can undergo training in adventure sports at the canton's expense; in France the UCPA Centres (Union Nationale des Centres Sportifs de Plein Air) give young adults the opportunity for a residential programme at a specialist centre at which they can undergo training in activities such as skiing, sea kayaking, canyoning or sailing. Generally the focus is on a single, specialist activity but there is a parallel importance given to social matters. This seems to be a highly effective way of reaching young adults at an important point of their development. In Belgium many kids between nine and twelve years will attend coastal centres offering 'zeeklassen' (sea classes), or go to a forested area for 'bosklassen' (forest classes), but fewer adolescents will have access to adventure activities.

In Britain, the more usual targets of open access adventure activities are pupils in their early teens. They tend to be offered multi-activity programmes with a considerable emphasis on personal and social skills and often little expectation that learners will continue to participate after their taste of a particular activity.

Some countries use adventure activities as a model for military style leadership and control (which were, in the guise of War Office Selection Boards important antecedents of modern adventure education) while others adopt a more philosophical or even mystical approach. In Scandinavia and most notably in Norway the Friluftsliv movement is important and influential and has, at its core, the relationship between individuals and wild places.

Friluftsliv seems to be a philosophy which is in direct descent from Rousseau and the Romantic movement and anyone engaged in outdoor education should acquaint themselves with its unique perspectives. I was privileged to join Nils Faarlund, one of its evangelists, on a ski tour when he was President of the Norwegian Mountain Guides. He tried to turn those of us who were present away from a narrow, goal-orientated view of mountains towards something more holistic – the skier/mountaineer as part of nature rather than as conqueror of nature, mountains as mystical manifestations and not mere commodities. He implored us to see our uphill ski tracks not just as a means to an end, but as a form of sculpture, of calligraphy, putting us into intimate contact with the shape of the land and the texture of the snow. We listened to silence, breathed in the wilderness, tried to understand the life of a willow grouse and escaped from all urgency of operation on a journey more internal than external.

Local effects

Every country will have individuals and small organisations that have seized on the valuable interaction between people and wild places. It would be surprising if these operations were not subject to similar constraints and distractions as those described elsewhere in this book, but it may be purely local expectations and local conditions that have the strongest influence on quality and safety. Small providers are more likely to be in tune with local conditions and customs but may be blind to hazards that they have grown up with.

When I visited a provider of adventure programmes in Finland I was impressed with what I saw and the way those taking part engaged with the superb forest environment. As a poor swimmer I may see the hazards of swimming in a somewhat exaggerated form, but I was surprised by how casually that activity was addressed. One is rarely far from a lake in Finland and it seemed that youngsters were allowed to swim much as they wished and without apparent precautions or supervision. In the UK this would not be judged acceptable practice and it would usually be expected that there be constraints relating to people swimming alone, to supervision from the shore and to the presence of lifesavers.

I gained the impression that such things were uncommon in Finland, because virtually every child there will have grown up in an environment where they are constantly in and out of water. Within this context it is easy to see that the precautions outlined above might be seen as ludicrous for a group of adolescents and perhaps as inappropriate as issuing body armour for a simple forest walk.

So should we expect the Finns to conform to the same expectations as a provider in Dorset? In my opinion we should certainly expect the same quality in the processes of risk assessment and risk management but we should not automatically expect the same outcome from these for what, after all, may be a substantially different client group. As long as the hazards of swimming had been considered for the target clients of the organisation and an appropriate level of control implemented as a result of a careful assessment by a responsible person, then we should be satisfied.

As with any arrangements for risk management there must be a willingness to review if, for example, a different client group are to be involved. Perhaps participants are to be younger or maybe a group from overseas is to attend. It is easy to see that a group from Dorset or Dubai may have entirely different capabilities and, more importantly, different expectations to a group who have grown up in Finland. Failure to anticipate such different capabilities and expectations can sow the seeds of serious problems; being alert to such possibilities is an important area of consideration for groups playing 'away matches' and working outside their normal area of operation.

Playing away

Some outdoor education providers operate on a truly international scale. Perhaps the most obvious example is Outward Bound®, which in 2006 has national operations in almost thirty countries. These conform to certain common requirements but each has a distinctly national character. In Sabah, participants on Outward Bound® programmes undertake jungle treks in tropical rain forests, in Finland journeys are made on skis, spending the nights in forest snow shelters. Given Belgium's national reputation for beer one can perhaps claim a unique national manifestation in the fact that the Ottward Bound® school near to Lustin owns its own cave, 'Le Trou Alexandre', to which entry is made through the back room of a local bar.

The metaphor of the journey is central in outdoor education and journeys to entirely new environments and unfamiliar cultures can be enormously powerful. Getting the proper balance between risk and security can be difficult enough in a familiar environment; to do the same overseas needs careful attention and plenty of good fortune. Travelling to a place where not all life's uncertainties are controlled is part of the challenge and value of the experience, but it generally means that a lower standard of security and control must be tolerated. Some honesty about this is desirable – it helps no one to pretend that the risks of a journey on foot across the Kalahari or a sailing voyage across the Indian Ocean can be brought to the same level as a local picnic.

This is no excuse for a careless approach; the best safety will always come from hazards recognised, faced and managed. Skilled field staff and careful preparation and planning can reduce the level of risk to one that is readily tolerable in the face of the benefits to be harvested. An effective approach is to establish a partnership with a provider in-country, so as to be able to plug into their local knowledge and support networks. When this is done, it is vital to avoid misunderstandings about the allocation of responsibility and about who has the final say in the event of a field emergency. Any basic difference in safety culture is likely to make itself known at the least convenient moment and perhaps when it is too late. Preparation, reconnaissance and dialogue with the local operator will help to avoid this.

In my experience, there is much to be said for overall control lying with the visiting leader since that person is (one hopes) familiar with the ethos and style of the venture, is more likely to be familiar with the participants and is less likely to have language difficulties in communicating with them. However, to have overall charge when one of your colleagues has greater local knowledge and more immediate expertise is not always a comfortable situation, and, in the event of difficulties, may call for a great deal of assertiveness. This should be included in the person specification for the field leader.

The field leader

The field leader is without doubt the most important influence on quality and safety and should ideally be a person of great self-sufficiency and maturity of attitude with the ability to solve problems in a creative and unflustered manner. The leader will usually operate within a framework of support and with a clear chain of responsibility, perhaps through another in-country colleague, to a focal point of contact supervision and support back in the country of origin. When children of both genders are in the party, this should be reflected in supervisory staffing. Consideration should be given to the possibilities of excessive fatigue for all involved in an expedition, and especially for leaders. A proper emergency response is more likely from a leader who is not suffering the cumulative effects of several days of sleep deprivation.

It is wise when planning to assume that things will not always go according to plan. Extreme weather, civil unrest and epidemics can destroy the best made plans but, although less dramatic, the constant attrition of unreliable communications, uncertain transport schedules and apparent unfamiliarity with any concept of urgency can be equally devastating. Communication and the flow of information needs careful attention but it is wise not to put too much trust in electronic technology. Satellite phones are fantastic devices but they do need to have battery power when you have to make that urgent call. Sometimes, one is forced back to the basic position where the field leader has to be trusted to make the best decision ... It is normally wise at all times for the leader to have ready access to contact details, including those for parents and guardians.

The standard approaches to assessing and managing risk will apply but will sometimes need modification in the face of harsh reality. When involved in the arrangements for an expedition to a tropical rain forest our initial decision was to adopt the practices that we would use for an extended wild country journey in Europe as our starting point. This worked well, up to a point. Some weeks later after an initial foray into the jungle one of our leaders pointed out that our operating principles required him to carry a warm sleeping bag for emergency use. 'It's about 35 Celsius in the middle of the night!' he squawked, and he was entirely correct in thinking that the sleeping bag was an irrelevance and no more than unnecessary extra weight.

Basic first aid may be the same all over the world, but expedition medicine may be unusually remote from specialist medical assistance and may also have to deal with unfamiliar illnesses and parasites. It is desirable for leaders to have training in the specifics of expedition medicine and for medical advice to be sought during the preparation phase on what might be encountered. Poisonous or aggressive wild animals, malaria, bilharzia, frostbite and altitude sickness may seem horrifying but an appropriate operational regime will often reduce the risk to a tolerable level.

First-aid kits will often require expansion to deal with the possibility of more extended treatment and may, under medical advice, need to be supplemented with some additional medications such as antibiotics, analgesics or equipment such as sterile injection kits.

In the event of serious illness or injury, evacuation from some regions can be laborious and uncertain and severe weather and rising rivers can cause further complications.

Differences of culture

Cultural differences and the revelations that they can bring are among the joys of travel but can also be the point of origin of conflict or hostility. Good manners dictate that we should avoid offending our hosts over matters of dress, behaviour, religious observance or forms of expression but in extreme forms such occurrences can lead to grave difficulties. Skimpy clothing or a flirtatious or even friendly manner can be misinterpreted as signals of sexual availability; assertiveness can come across as aggression. A sensitive approach and training in how to avoid the escalation of conflict are worth consideration.

Differences of legal system

Litigation in the event of personal injury in organised outdoor activities appears to be much more likely to ensue in the United States and the United Kingdom than in other countries, but it is unwise to assume that immunity exists anywhere. Some countries do limit the amount of personal injury claims and this can reduce the level of insurance premiums. For overseas expeditions it should be borne in mind that a litigant may be able choose to have an action heard under the legal system of the country in which the injury occurred, the country of the injured party or, in the case of large international operations, in the country of its headquarters. Professional advice is desirable, but, as always, the best policy is to minimise the chance of serious incidents by putting maximum effort into preparation, planning and quality leadership.

Some countries have specific legislation relating to adventure activities although this is often held in abeyance in the case of voluntary groups or school parties. In Britain, anybody can advertise themselves as, for instance, a 'mountain guide'. An unqualified person may run into deep waters in the event of litigation following personal injury to a client, but the law does not prevent their operation in the first place. In contrast, the alpine countries tend to have rather strict legislation in this area so that the profession of mountain guide is subject to the prescriptions of the law in much the same way as the professions of medicine or engineering. It is wise to ensure that one is not inadvertently, or otherwise, in breach of these laws. Swiss and French courts have been known to imprison guides who have been judged negligent and unqualified guides have been intercepted and arrested by policemen in helicopters suddenly appearing in the snowy wastes of the Vallée Blanche on Mont Blanc.

When planning an overseas venture it is unwise to assume that legal requirements on providers will be the same. Seat belts in vehicles is a near automatic provision in some countries, in others it is not and organisers may suddenly discover that the transport that they have arranged in advance is in the back of an open truck …

Chapter summary

- Outdoor education exists internationally in many forms.
- When operating abroad it is important to identify any conflicts between visitors' expectations and local practices.
- Intrinsic levels of risk are often higher in remote overseas expeditions.
- Cultural and legal differences can be important.

Recommended books and sources

Outdoor education

Drasdo, Harold (1972) *Education and the Mountain Centres*. Tyddyn Gabriel.

Duke of Edinburgh's Award (2000) *Duke of Edinburgh's Award Handbook*. Duke of Edinburgh Award.

English Outdoor Council (2006) *High Quality Outdoor Education*. English Outdoor Council.

Exeter, David (ed.) (2001) *Learning in the Outdoors*. Outward Bound Trust.

Hopkins, David and Putnam, Roger (2003) *Personal Growth through Adventure*. David Fulton.

Hunt, John (ed.) (1989) *In Search of Adventure*. Talbot Adair Press.

Keay, Wally (2000) *Expedition Guide*. Duke of Edinburgh's Award.

Mortlock, Colin (1984) *The Adventure Alternative*. Cicerone Press.

Risk and its management

Adams, John (1995) *Risk*. UCL Press.

DfEE (1998) *Health and Safety of Pupils on Educational Visits*. DfEE.

Furedi, Frank (1998) *Culture of Fear*. Cassell.

Haddock, Cathye (1993) *Managing Risks in Outdoor Activities*. New Zealand Mountain Safety Council.

Health and Safety Executive (1996) *Guidance to the Licensing Authority on the Adventure Activities Licensing Regulations 1996*. HSE.

Health and Safety Executive (1999a) *Adventure Activities Centres: Five Steps to Risk Assessment*. HSE.

Health and Safety Executive (1999b) *Five Steps to Risk Assessment*. HSE.

Health and Safety Executive (1999c) *Reducing Error and Influencing Behaviour*. HSE.

Leemon, Drew and Schimelpfenig, Tod (2005) *Risk Management for Outdoor Leaders*. National Outdoor Leadership School.

Pratt, Jeremy (2003) *Human Factors and Flight Safety*, Private Pilot Licence Course, Vol. 5. AFE Paperback.

Reason, James (1990) *Human Error*. Cambridge University Press.

Reason, James (1997) *Managing the Risks of Organisational Accidents*. Ashgate.

Leadership

Adair, John (1989) *Effective Leadership*. Gower.

Barr, L. and Barr, N. (1989) *The Leadership Equation*. Eakin Press.

MLTE (n.d.) *MLTE Remote Supervision Guidance Notes*. Mountain Leader Training England.

Ogilvie, Ken (2005) *Leading and Managing Groups in the Outdoors*. Institute of Outdoor Learning.

Ramblers' Association (1994) Navigation and Leadership. Ramblers' Association.

Activity specific

Barton, Bob and Wright, Blyth (2000) *A Chance in a Million? Scottish Avalanches.* Scottish Mountaineering Club.

British Canoe Union (2002) *Canoe and Kayak Handbook*. British Canoe Union.

British Mountaineering Council (1998) *BMC Climbing Wall Manual*. BMC.

Bruce, Peter (2004) *Adlard Coles' Heavy Weather Sailing*. Adlard Coles.

Ferrero, Franco (1998) *White Water Safety and Rescue*. Pesda Press.

Fyffe, Alan and Peter, Iain (1997) *The Handbook of Climbing*. Pelham Books.

Hiscock, Eric (1991) *Cruising under Sail*. Adlard Coles.

Langmuir, Eric (1995) *Mountaincraft and Leadership*. SSC/MLTB.

Long, Steve (2003) *Hillwalking*, Mountain Leader Training Handbook. MLTUK.

Mason, Bill (2001) *Path of the Paddle*. Cordee.

MLTUK (various authors) *Mountain Leader Training Handbooks*. MLTUK (covering hillwalking, rock climbing, winter mountaineering, etc.).

Nealy, William (1990) *Kayak – A Manual of Technique*. Menasha Ridge Press.

Nealy, William (1992) *Mountain Bike – A Manual of Beginning to Advanced Technique*. Menasha Ridge Press.

Peter, Libby (2005) *Rock Climbing*, Mountain Leader Training Handbook. MLTUK.

Adventure

Bonington, Chris (2000) *The Quest for Adventure*. Weidenfeld & Nicholson Illustrated.

Diemberger, Kurt (1971) *Summits and Secrets*. Allen & Unwin.

Hawkridge, John (1991) *Uphill All the Way*. Michael Joseph.

Knox-Johnston, Robin (1994) *A World of My Own*. W. W. Norton.

Murray, W. H. (1979) *Moutaineering in Scotland*. Diadem.

Tilman, Bill (1958) *Mischief in Patagonia*. Cambridge University Press.

Whymper, Edward (1981) *Scrambles Amongst the Alps in Years 1860–69*. Ten Speed.

Wilson, Brian (1998) *Blazing Paddles*. Wildland Press.

Websites

AALA: http://www.aala.org

British Canoe Union: http://www.bcu.org.uk

British Mountaineering Council: http://www.thebmc.co.uk

Campaign for Adventure: http://www.campaignforadventure.org

Department for Education and Skills (UK): http://www.dfes.gov.uk

Duke of Edinburgh's Award: http://www.theaward.org

Health and Safety Executive: http://www.hse.gov.uk/schooltrips/facts.htm

Institute for Outdoor Learning: http://www.outdoor-learning.org

Marine Accident Investigation Branch: http://www.maib.dft.gov.uk

Mountain Leader Training UK: http://www.mltuk.org

OB International: http://www.outwardbound.net/index.php

OB Trust: http://www.outwardbound-uk.org

Outdoor Education Advisors' Panel: http://www.oeap.info/index.htm

Ramblers' Association: http://www.ramblers.org.uk

Royal Yachting Association: http://www.rya.org.uk

Teachernet: http://www.teachernet.gov.uk

Wilderdom: http://www.wilderdom.com

Bibliography

Adventure Activities Advisory Committee (2006) *Surviving a Career in Adventure Activities* (document awaiting publication).

Adair, J. (1973) *Action-Centred Leadership*. Aldershot: Gower.

Adams, J. (1995) *Risk*. London: UCL Press.

Bailie, M. (2003) *Lessons Learned from Stainforth Beck?* Available online at: http://www.outdoor-learning.org/news/stainforthbeck.htm.

Barton, R. (1998) Unpublished internal documents for Outward Bound Trust.

Bunyan, N. (2001) *Scout Chief Cleared over Death of Boy on Snowdon*. Available online at: http://www.telegraph.co.uk/news/main.jhtml?xml=/news/2001/10/17/nfall17.xml.

Canadian Mountain Holidays (CMH) (2006) *Safety and Waiver*. Available online at: http://www.canadianmountainholidays.com/ski/safety_waiver/waiver.

de Geuss, A. (1991) Unpublished address at Outward Bound® International conference, Aberdovey.

Denning, Lord (1968) in *Hucks* v. *Cole*; reported in [1993] 4 Med LR 393, 396 CA.

DfES (2002) *Standards for LEAs in Overseeing Educational Visits*. London: DfES.

DfES (2006) *Lords' Select Committee on Economic Affairs: Inquiry into the Government's Policy on Risk Management. Memorandum submitted by the Department for Education and Skills*. London: DfES.

Duke of Edinburgh's Award (2000) *Duke of Edinburgh's Award Handbook*. Windsor: Duke of Edinburgh's Award.

HSE (1996) *Guidance to the Licensing Authority on the Adventure Activities Licensing Regulations 1996*. London: HSE Books.

HSE (1999) *Five Steps to Risk Assessment*. London: HSE Books.

HSE (2005) *School Trips – Glenridding Beck*. Available online at: http://www.hse.gov.uk/schooltrips/.

Hersey, P. and Blanchard, K. H. (1977) *The Management of Organizational Behaviour*, 3rd edn. Upper Saddle River, NJ: Prentice Hall.

Hoagin, R. (1970) *Reconnaissance on an Educational Frontier*. Oxford: Oxford University Press.

Hogan, J. M. (1968) *Impelled into Experiences: The Story of the Outward Bound® Schools*. Educational Productions Ltd.

Jamieson, B. and Geldsetzer, T. (1996) *Avalanche Accidents in Canada*, Vol. 4. British Columbia: Canadian Avalanche Association.

Johnston, P. (2000) *Firms Face Tougher Law on Disaster Negligence*. Available online at: http://www.telegraph.co.uk/htmlContent.jhtml?html=/archive/2000/05/23/nneg23.html.

Knight, S. (2000) *The Safe Outdoors*. Available online at: http://www.spiked-online.co.uk/Articles/0000000053B8.htm.

Knight, S. and Anderson, D. (2005) *Why Outdoor Adventure?* Available online at: http://www.generationyouthissues.org.uk/outdoor_adventure.htm.

Kolb, D. A. (1984) *Experiential Learning: Experience as the Source of Learning and Development.* Englewood Cliffs, NJ: Prentice Hall.

Leemon, D. and Schimelpfenig, T. (2003) 'Wilderness injury, illness, and evacuation: National Outdoor Leadership School's incident profiles, 1999–2002', *Wilderness Environ. Med.*, 14 (3): 174–82.

McCammon, I. (2002) *Evidence of Heuristic Traps in Recreational Avalanche Incidents.* Paper presented to the International Snow Science Workshop, British Columbia: International Snow Science Workshop.

McNair J, in *Bolam v. Friern Hospital Management Committee* [1957] 1 WLR 583, 587.

MAIB (Marine Accident Investigation Branch) (1999) *Report of the Investigation of the Capsize of a School Boat on Fountain Lake, Portsmouth with the Loss of One Life on 16 September 1999*, Report No. 6/2001.

MAIB (Marine Accident Investigation Branch) (2000) *Report of the Investigation of a Man Overboard Fatality from the Etchells 22 Keelboat* Wahoo *off Yarmouth, Isle of Wight on 14 May 1999*, File 1/10/191.

MAIB (Marine Accident Investigation Branch) (2005) *Report on the Investigation of the Brenscombe Outdoor Centre Canoe Swamping Accident in Poole Harbour, Dorset on 6 April 2005*, Report No. 22/2005.

Mortlock, C. (1978) *Adventure Education* (monograph published by the author).

Mountain 20 (1972) *The Cairngorm Tragedy*, reproduced in *The Games Climbers Play* (1978), Diadem.

Neave, H. (1990) *The Deming Dimension*. Knoxville, TN: SPC Press.

OBI (2004) *Outward Bound® International Safety Review Manual – Guidelines for Conducting Safety Review*, OBI ed. Ian Wade. Salt Lake City, UT: Outward Bound® International.

Price, T. (1966) *Address to the Royal Society of Arts*. London: Royal Society of Arts.

Scottish Executive (2005) *Health and Safety on Educational Excursions – A Good Practice Guide*. Edinburgh: Scottish Executive.

Sheen, B. (1987) *MV Herald of Free Enterprise: Report of Court No. 8074 Formal Investigation*. London: HMSO for Department of Transport.

Stoner, J. A. F. (1961) 'A comparison of individual and group decisions involving risk'. Unpublished Master's thesis, Massachusetts Institute of Technology.

Williamson, J. and Meyer, D. (2003) *Potential Causes of Accidents in Outdoor Pursuits* in *Wilderness Risk Management* (2003), Wyoming: The National Outdoor Leadership School.

Index